THE
REALITY AND THE
RHETORIC

Organisational sustainability reporting

Geoff Frost

Stewart Jones

Philip Lee

SYDNEY UNIVERSITY PRESS

Published 2013 by Sydney University Press
SYDNEY UNIVERSITY PRESS
University of Sydney Library
sydney.edu.au/sup

Sydney University Press
Fisher Library F03
University of Sydney NSW 2006 AUSTRALIA
Email: sup.info@sydney.edu.au

National Library of Australia Cataloguing-in-Publication entry
Author: Frost, Geoffrey R
Title: The reality and the rhetoric : organisational sustainability
         reporting / Geoff Frost; Stewart Jones; Philip Lee
ISBN: 9781743320167 (paperback)
Notes: Includes index
Subjects: Sustainable development reporting--Australia
         Economic development--Environmental aspects--Australia
         Environmental policy--Australia
Other Authors/Contributors:
         Jones, Stewart, author
         Lee, Philip John, author
Dewey Number: 338.0994

Cover design by Dushan Mrva-Montoya

Contents

About the authors

Geoff Frost

Geoff Frost is an associate professor in the Discipline of Accounting, the University of Sydney Business School. He has researched and co-authored many scholarly articles on reporting and accounting of sustainability activities, the accountant's role in the environmental management system, and the use of alternative reporting mediums by reporting entities.

Stewart Jones

Stewart Jones is a professor of accounting at the University of Sydney, specialising in corporate financial reporting. Over the past decade he has published over 100 scholarly works in financial reporting and accounting, including nearly 60 refereed articles, ten books, and numerous book chapters, working papers and short monographs.

Stewart's research interests include sustainability reporting, credit risk and corporate distress analysis, accounting theory, standard setting, international standards harmonisation, financial analysis and research methodology. Stewart is currently Editor-in-Chief of the prestigious international quarterly *Abacus*. Stewart's industry experience includes the interpretation of accounting standards, financial analysis and regulation, credit risk modelling and corporate performance analysis.

Philip Lee

Philip Lee is professor of finance and accounting at the SP Jain School of Global Management in Sydney, Australia. Prior to this appointment, he worked as an associate professor of accounting at the University of Sydney. Philip now has more than 20 years' experience in providing management education.

Philip's interest in financial markets and financial reporting encompass sustainability reporting. Forming Sustainability Australia with his co-authors, he has embarked on benchmarking some of the best practices in sustainability reporting in Australia. Philip has also co-authored many scholarly articles within the field of financial reporting, as well as a leading textbook for financial statement analysis.

Overview of the project

The reality and the rhetoric: organisational sustainability reporting is the result of a collaborative ARC Linkage project between the University of Sydney and CPA Australia. The project strives to provide an understanding of avenues available for the accounting profession and business organisations to more formally embrace the management of environmental and social aspects of organisational performance.

Initially informed by earlier work commissioned by CPA Australia on the social environmental reporting practices of Australian companies, the project undertook a case study approach to investigate the underlying processes and systems organisations are developing to support both the external reporting and management of social and environmental performance. The focus is therefore on internal sustainability information gathering and reporting processes and the use of that information by internal decision makers. Against this background, the project had the following specific aims:

- To evaluate the existing systems and procedures that are used to generate data on non-financial performance – including physical/environmental, socio-economic and governance concepts – to help overcome obstacles and resistance to sustainability reporting

- To explore ways in which sustainability data can be collected efficiently and better integrated through the accounting system, how accounting systems could be extended to incorporate such information, and the tools required to complete these specifications

- To understand how internal management and decision makers in organisations make use of sustainability information and how the data might be enhanced by expanded accounting systems

- To understand how sustainability reporting can be improved at a substantive level for external users in the areas of disclosure and verification
- To provide a basis for developing reporting regulations and guidelines.

METHODOLOGY

The study consists of five case organisations – Green Insurer, Herbal Life, Local Leader, Clear Water and Infrastructor. Each organisation is diverse, and has been chosen to help provide insight on:

- Industry – underlying operations and activities (finance sector, construction, water, local government, and manufacturing/ pharmaceutical)
- Size – while all are 'large' organisations, they range from multinational to local government (10,000+ employees to a couple of hundred)
- Regulatory environment – sample includes listed companies, an unlisted subsidiary of a multinational corporation, local government and state government authority.

The organisations involved were initially approached through the office of chief financial officer (CFO). As an accounting study it is important to have the accountants 'buy' into the project from the outset. Once access was gained, interviews were undertaken with any staff member deemed to have a significant association with the development, reporting or use of sustainability data. The interviewees included: accountants, HR managers, procurement, systems managers, sustainability managers and senior executives. The cases sought to understand the flow of information from when data is first collected in the organisation to when it is used. For example, for one organisation interviews were held with the foreman on the factory floor who designed the data collection protocols for packaging and waste. For all five organisations the CFO was interviewed, for two the chief executive officer (CEO) was interviewed. In total across the five case study organisations approximately 100 people were interviewed.

A significant amount of documentation on sustainability was also collected. Initially this included the information that was publicly available and which was used to support the choice of case study. Through the process of undertaking the case studies additional documentation was collected.

THE CASE STUDY ORGANISATIONS

Finance company – Green Insurer

The finance company that took part in the project is listed as a top 40 company on the Australian stock exchange. It is a multinational corporation with significant operations in the UK and New Zealand, as well as operations throughout Asia. The company has a reputation as a leader in sustainability reporting, being one of the more prominent Australian companies to support the use of the global reporting initiative (GRI). It has been a leading reporter of sustainability for a number of years. The company's sustainability report includes considerable performance data. Under the direction of an executive with a high profile in the sustainability community, the company has been developing internal systems with the ultimate aim of embedding sustainability key performance indicators (KPIs) in individual performances. Due to a number of barriers, the sustainability information system is being developed in parallel to existing information systems.

Manufacturing/pharmaceutical – Herbal Life

The manufacturing/pharmaceutical company that took part in the project is a listed Australian company with a market capitalisation of between $200 million and $400 million. The company only provides limited external disclosure of sustainability information. Their annual report contained no more than two to four pages of sustainability information, and no significant information is available through other sources. Despite the limited availability of performance information provided, the company enjoys a high reputation as a socially responsible organisation. This may partly be due to the organisation's branding. It is the branding that is influential in strategic decisions of the organisation. For example, recent rapid growth had necessitated a move to larger premises. The relocation was influenced most significantly by the welfare of existing employees rather than minimising the total capital outlay. The information systems within the organisation (outside accounting and manufacturing) are primitive compared to many comparable organisations. However, despite the lack of KPIs on social issues, sustainability factors are considered when decisions are being made within the organisation.

Local government – Local Leader

The local government that took part in the project is perceived as a leader in sustainability management and reporting. It is actively involved in a number of initiatives on sustainability reporting. At the commencement of data collection the organisation provided a template on environmental accounting for local governments. The organisation has produced a sustainability report for a number of years. The councillors and management have adopted a position that sustainability must be backed by action, with council driving the construction of new six-star Green buildings. Within the organisation there is tension between the commercial realities of a modern local government and an organisation which seeks to meet the needs of the community. Limited resources with underdeveloped and undefined management processes can be compared to extensive external reporting.

Water authority – Clear Water

The water authority involved in the project has the responsibility to maintain water supply for four million people. It is a state-owned authority. The organisation has produced a sustainability report for a number of years for which it has won reporting awards. Clear Water is noted for its innovative sustainability reporting. Internally, the organisation employs a considerable number of technical experts, many of whom have independently developed systems to gather and analyse data for their own purposes. To better enable executives and the board to understand the context of sustainability, the organisation has been undergoing a data warehousing process. What was initially envisaged to take a few months has dragged out over years.

Construction/mining – Infrastructor

The construction/mining entity involved in the project is an unlisted subsidiary of a multinational corporation, ultimately based in Europe. The organisation prides itself on being a leader in sustainability, which is used to differentiate it from other subsidiaries and the parent entity. In construction it is active in pursuing green standards for Infrastructor projects. In the mining operations clients are pushing for improved performance on environmental issues. The business model is based on projects, which affects the continuity of knowledge from one project to the next. The organisation has been developing a knowledge database for best practice management which includes sustainability issues. While the organisation is active in the management of sustainability issues, this is not evident in the external reporting and is occurring outside the domain of the organisation's accountants.

OUTLINE OF QUESTIONS FOR RESPONDENTS

The interviews were semi-structured and focused mainly on the organisations' sustainability management systems. Participants were interviewed across a broad range of issues and interview questions were adapted to the contextual background, position, and experience of each respondent interviewed. Appendix 1 provides an overview of the research instrument. Most interviews commenced with an initial explanatory overview of the research project as well as an outline of the purpose for the research. Respondents were then invited to discuss their background and specific role performed within the organisation. Several of the interview questions were focused on the following:

• How sustainability information was collected and reported within the organisation

• The types of sustainability data collected across the different divisions

• How data was measured and reported

• The types of information systems used to collect data

• The timing and frequency of sustainability reporting

• The role of sustainability data in internal decision-making

• How well the internal sustainability data is integrated with internal accounting systems

• The auditing and assurance of sustainability data.

Other interview questions related to stakeholder engagement as well as the particular hurdles the organisation faces with respect to the collection, integration and reporting of sustainability data.

A case study analysis of Green Insurer

Background of Green Insurer

At the time interviews were conducted, Green Insurer operated a portfolio of general insurance businesses in Australia, New Zealand, Asia and the UK, including some of Australia's leading general insurance brands. Insurance products are sold under the Green Insurer business model:

- directly to customers through both branch and agency networks throughout Australia as well as via call centres and online facilities
- indirectly to customers through intermediary channels, including insurance brokers, authorised representatives, motor dealerships and financial institutions.

At time of the interviews, Green Insurer was an ASX 100 listed company, having around 950,000 shareholders, 16,000 employees and a market capitalisation of around $8 billion.

Green Insurer's corporate strategy continues to focus on creating a portfolio of 'high performing, customer-focused, diverse operations providing general insurance in a manner that delivers superior experiences for stakeholders and creates shareholder value.'

Regulatory environment of Green Insurer

General insurers in Australia are subject to a significant amount of regulation. There is the corporate regulatory regime that applies to Australian incorporated businesses, as well as a range of industry-specific regulations at the federal, state and territory levels. These regulations cover prudential supervision, market conduct and consumer protection requirements. However Green Insurer is under no particular statutory requirements to produce sustainability information or reports.

Why Green Insurer was selected for a case study

Green Insurer was selected as a case study because of its established corporate reputation as a leader in the sustainability field. It is also differentiated from other respondents insofar as it is an ASX 100 public company with significant international business operations (particularly in Asia, the UK and New Zealand). Green Insurer is recognised as an industry leader in the financial modelling of the potential climate change impacts of global warming. The company is well known for having adopted a number sustainability policies and initiatives which are supported by senior executives (a 'top down' approach) as well as employees. For instance, Green Insurer is one of the largest users of hybrid vehicles (Toyota Prius) in Australia. The company also claims to be an innovator in some 'green' insurance products and services. At the time of the interviews, Green Insurer had published three sustainability reports on its company website and incorporated some limited sustainability information into its annual report. The company publishes a range of environmental, community and employee-related sustainability indicators in its sustainability report. Green Insurer is also unique for seeking to become carbon neutral by 2012 and has instituted a number of sustainability initiatives within the organisation to achieve this objective.

Respondents selected for the case study

Respondents were drawn from a wide cross-section of Green Insurer staff, and 16 interviews were conducted, averaging approximately one hour each. Interviews were held with a number senior managers, divisional heads and internal consultants, including: consultant for corporate social responsibility; senior management accountant, shared services; manager, analytics and reporting; manager, workforce, reporting and analysis, culture and reputation;

procurement manager; manager, innovation and sustainability; group head of sustainable business practices; acting senior manager, group risk assurance; management information, PI CFO; senior manager, sustainable business practices; manager, group statutory reporting and consolidation; group chief financial officer; consultant, sustainable business practices; chief risk officer and group actuary; head of group treasury and finance; CEO, asset management and reinsurance; and a divisional sustainability manager.

Outline of case study

The remainder of this case analysis is organised as follows:

Section one explores some of the issues surrounding the public image of sustainability projected by Green Insurer and the perceptions of sustainability reporting by respondents working daily with the programs and initiatives within the organisation.

Section two explores Green Insurer's processes, systems and methodologies for the collection, integration and reporting of sustainability information.

Section three explores the extent to which stakeholder engagement influences or impacts on sustainability reporting practices within the organisation.

Section four discusses potential hurdles confronting the collection, integration and reporting of sustainability information with the organisation.

Finally, some conclusions and policy implications are considered.

SECTION ONE

Public image versus internal perceptions

While Green Insurer embraced the sustainability initiative as corporate strategy quite recently (at the time of the interviews), a wide cross-section of respondents indicated very strong support for the various sustainability initiatives, policies and strategies employed. Although the viewpoints of respondents differed quite significantly on some issues, the interviews revealed a strong underlying sense of enthusiasm and commitment to the concept of sustainability overall and the general strategic direction Green Insurer was taking on the issue. As stated by one respondent, there seemed to be a natural fit between sustainability and the overarching business goals of an insurance company. The consultant for corporate social responsibility stated: 'Being an insurance company, we look forward, we're very future-focused and sustainability is all about looking forward so there's a lovely kind of cultural fit there.' For instance, Green Insurer's financial modelling of the potential impacts of global warming (such as changing with weather and tidal patterns) is perhaps among the most sophisticated in the industry.

Green Insurer has a strong reputation in sustainability, having won numerous awards in the 2006–07 financial year. The company's sustainability report has been developed around the Global Reporting Initiative (GRI) Sustainability Reporting Guidelines Version 3.0. Several respondents acknowledged that these guidelines are the internationally accepted best practice measurement system for social, environmental and economic reporting.

Green Insurer's corporate website identifies numerous stakeholder groups in the preparation of its sustainability report, which include customers, shareholders, employees, government bodies and regulators, suppliers, unions, community partners, business organisations, and industry groups. For instance, with respect to the supply chain, Green Insurer claims it is working on the challenge of establishing consistent sustainability principles in supplier partnerships.

The company also claims to have delivered some 'green' products and services for customers that align with their position on sustainability. Green Insurer's website states:

> First and foremost, these are customer offers that make business sense, but they also reflect a new way of thinking for the long-term about how our customers respond to innovative new offers that are right for the 21st century.

For instance, to encourage fuel-efficient cars, customers can receive a ten per cent saving on comprehensive car insurance.

Internally, most respondents appeared to recognise the importance of sustainability to the organisation as a whole. Many respondents not only supported the philosophy of sustainability but also perceived a strong business case for sustainability. For example, the manager of innovation and sustainability stated:

> I do think that things like the Dow Jones and those other global reporting initiatives and all of those other big indicators ... are of increasing importance to us because we are starting to understand that that opens up a new set of investors who are potentially interested in Green Insurer.

A number of respondents also appeared deeply committed to the underlying philosophy of sustainability. The manager of innovation and sustainability stated:

> It's definitely an issue in that we obviously take a very public stand on all of this stuff and we need to be seen to be consistent ... that's really the reason why I do what I do because, I mean,

let's face it, if Green Insurer doesn't do anything with its environmental footprint, it's really not going to make any difference to climate change overall. But we do it because it's important for us to be doing things consistent with the message that we're putting out there very strongly. It's very much the same in all of the areas, and in some of the areas I think it takes probably a bit longer to understand what that means.

There is no doubt that, to a larger extent, Green Insurer is putting 'its money where its mouth is' in regards to sustainability. A number of respondents observed that Green Insurer was adopting a range of interesting and innovative sustainability initiatives and was seriously committed to these practices. A good example of how the organisation influenced environmental practice with respect to the building it leases is described by the chief risk officer and group actuary:

This building you're sitting in … is an interesting illustration because it is a bit unusual. Just over a year ago now, we basically got to the end of our first ten year lease in this building and we are the only tenant now. So we had an interesting discussion with our landlord, which went something along the lines of, 'Well, we don't have to stay here. There are two or three other brand new buildings out there that are five-star green buildings and they'll cost us a lot less to run in electricity and water etc. particularly electricity for air-conditioning and lighting. If you want us to stay here and sign another ten year lease, you've got to basically refit this building so that it reaches the highest possible Green Star rating you can get.' And it turned out that they could get to about four and a half. They couldn't quite make it to five for all sorts of reasons. But what it did do, it dramatically dropped the cost of the energy used in the building and it was completely refitted with lights and switches that make the lights go off after a certain period of non-movement and all that sort of stuff. All the bathrooms have been redone to be much lower usage of water etc.

The bottom line, what actually happened is that even though ... they had to invest $25 million in the building to make that all happen, the landlord I mean, we came out with a total cost to us as the tenant, including all of the energy costs that we pay, basically slightly lower than the old lease when we started for the next lease. So we came out in front and the building came out in front if I could put it that way and the landlord was happy, because they didn't have an empty building.

Notwithstanding the seemingly strong cultural and senior executive support for sustainability within the organisation, it became clear from several respondents that Green Insurer's public image of sustainability (as projected in the sustainability and annual reports) was still some distance from the reality of how this information was perceived internally and applied in a practical way for decision-making. Some respondents indicated that the organisation was still struggling with the traditional business model focus on maximising returns, and how to balance financial priorities with its relatively new focus on sustainability.

Such conflicts were hinted at by the chief risk officer and group actuary who, while perceiving a tension between shareholder demands and sustainability, saw a strong underlying business case for sustainability. He stated:

Clearly the organisation is having a hard year and let's be fairly honest about that. That's fairly public. Having said that, I think there is a fairly deep seated belief in that [sustainability] principle in the organisation and it resonated very well with the mutual culture, I think it would be fair to say. It is quite motivating for employees to feel that they work for an organisation that takes some of this stuff seriously. There is no doubt there is a very significant business issue for us in the whole climate change debate, both on the liability side with paying claims but also on the assets side. It is a real business issue from our point of view. I don't think that's going to go away, if I can put it that way. Things obviously get more or less emphasis over time maybe, but just keeping shareholders happy has obviously got high emphasis at the moment. I don't think that means sustainability's going to disappear.

Some prominent senior executives expressed reservations about the overall direction Green Insurer was taking with sustainability. In terms of Green Insurer's recent restructure and repositioning on sustainability, the group chief financial officer brought out the tensions between Green Insurer's public image and the reality of sustainability within the organisation. This respondent highlighted the need to define what sustainability really means to the organisation, and particularly how the concept of sustainability needs to be embedded at the business unit level to have any organisational impact (rather than at the corporate level):

My personal view is that it hasn't been successful and we've lacked traction and my summary would be fantastic at 'the what' but not 'the how', in summary. We have over-engineered 'the what' to within an inch of its life. We did the press piece really well, talked to the world about how wonderful we were in doing all of this stuff and we have probably got about a

30 per cent track record would be my mark ... and I think it failed because it was led too much by the corporate office and owned too much by the corporate office, and it hasn't been owned by the business units so it's not embedded.

There has also been a confused message about what sustainability means. Too many emails going around about planting trees, not enough going around about sustainable profit going forward and the survival of the business for the long term, because this is really 'over the horizon thinking'. We haven't really got that message through. So that's my view.

As far as the restructure goes, I think you'll see that it will move quite a bit more before it settles. We're trying to move to a devolved model where more and more of the decisions are made by the people that are closest to the customers. That means devolving a whole lot of decision-making to the business units and a whole lot of tasks to the business units. Whenever you do that in an organisation of this size, you necessarily go through a phase where the expertise is moving away from the centre, along with the tasks hopefully. Otherwise you're delegating things to do to people who don't have the capability and you run the risk that the whole place slows down and goes through a trough. So we're in the process of refining expertise at the moment. We've been moving to the devolved model slowly over the last 18 months and I suspect that that is going to accelerate. Now that's not bad news for sustainability. It's actually good news for sustainability because I haven't spoken to any of the leaders of those business units that don't agree that it has a role in how they run their business. It's just the Green Insurer version of it will probably change and it will morph from an emphasis on community, to an emphasis on the organisation's performance and that's probably a good thing for everybody.

In terms of impacts, other respondents believed Green Insurer's sustainability drive would not have substantive societal impacts until they started developing more innovative 'green' insurance products and services (rather than just 'glossy' reports). The CEO, asset management and reinsurance made a colourful case for the development of more substantive 'green' insurance products. He stated: 'We should basically be saying, "you know we charge $1000 for a car on average [insurance]. If you're a Prius driver it's $500", not take ten per cent off. We should be driving really radical policies now.' And further:

> I have an idea and it's a really simple idea but boy it works well and it does a whole bunch of things ... So my idea is to sell an insurance policy with a carbon credit attached to it. I drive a Mini, so it will be a very small carbon credit, but it will be a carbon credit all the same. And that we say is that carbon credit is part of your policy and what you're doing is you're essentially offsetting your driving. So my Mini it's X amount per year and so on and so forth, so you've got people paying for it upfront. We would then turn around and say, rather like a no claims bonus – in my case I drive 10,000 kilometres a year let's say – if you commit to making that five thousand kilometres we will essentially pay for the carbon credit so you get your carbon credit for free. Now to me, there's a couple of things. Number one, being lazy like I am, I can have all my feelings around sustainability and I don't have to do anything like hand money over. It's almost something I get for free despite the fact I pay for it. But number two, which is much

more powerful for me, it offsets – it actually makes us a more profitable organisation, because having me on the road for only 50 per cent of the time clearly minimises the risk of me having a crash.

Furthermore, several respondents were concerned about how well Green Insurer was really performing in terms of its underlying sustainability systems and processes. In this context, Green Insurer's sustainability drive (at the time of the interviews) was battling against a number of internal setbacks and misadventures. The senior manager of sustainable business practices described some of these problems as follows:

Did we publish what we got last year? I don't think we did. I think we got a C or a C–, and that was last year, because of everything that went wrong … What we decided to do for this year was to clean up the problems with the systems and processes which had happened from last year's dramas and not look to too many new indicators. But we've been talking to the Expert Community Advisory Committee, which is the independent body to advise the company and they are quite good about it and they've gone away to come up with what indicators they'd like us to look at in 2009, because we need them now if we're going to start reporting from 1 July.

Other internal problems and issues that were impacting on sustainability reporting within the organisation included staff turnover, lack of maintenance of management systems to collect data, out-of-date guidelines and a general lack in coordination. The senior manager of sustainable business practices stated:

There was a lot of staff turnover, there were people who had gone on leave, maternity leave and other leave, and there hadn't been a great pickup of making this work. So we had, for example, the sustainability management guidelines, which you know, you've got to make people responsible for indicators. That was out of date, people didn't know they should have been providing data, there had been no follow up. This one poor person on their own was meant to bring it all together and they had a nervous breakdown. So that's essentially what happened. And it was awful ... it was that the system failed. So the management system, which you so desperately need, hadn't been maintained. And a lot of the communications hadn't happened. So the first thing we've done this year is to have a workshop with all the indicator owners, telling them their responsibilities. We put the executive in front of them, telling that this is what's happening this year, this is what's important, and what we've also instituted. Instead of just collecting the data after 30 June, we're now doing quarterly reporting.

While Green Insurer has a large number of interesting and innovative sustainability initiatives, there still appears to be a gap between the public image projected in the corporate reporting and the reality of sustainability within the organisation. For instance, while Green Insurer highlighted the G3 sustainability reporting guidelines as the benchmark for best practice, it was obvious from many respondents that actual reporting against the G3 was quite limited. Respondents did note, however, that the organisation published information on its environmental performance, including environmental indicators such as CO_2 emissions, electricity usage, fuel consumption, paper usage and air travel. Green Insurer also published customer satisfaction data and employee data, such as staff turnover, absenteeism and the number of woman in senior management and executive positions.

Several respondents observed that the G3's emphasis on materiality was the most important change affecting Green Insurer. The group head of sustainable business practices stated:

> I mean, we're really glad about the fact there are actually less indicators overall. There's more emphasis on materiality. I think that's actually the most important single change of G3. I must admit, I couldn't go through each of the indicators, chapter and verse.

Despite efforts to report against the G3, an external audit for the 2006–07 financial year highlighted numerous areas where Green Insurer was not reporting or was only partially reporting. This appears to be because many indicators identified in the G3 are not regarded as useful or appropriate to an insurance company.

The public image of sustainability appears to be divergent from internal perceptions in supplier sustainability performance reporting. Respondents noted that many of Green Insurer's larger 'corporate' suppliers have sustainability goals built into their supplier performance reports. According to Green Insurer's sustainability reports, 23 per cent of suppliers (accounting for 49 per cent of total supplier spend for the corporate suppliers) have these provisions. These suppliers cover areas such as employee relations, environmental responsibility and community engagement. Green Insurer recently sent 50 national suppliers and 350 smash repair businesses in New Zealand a Guide to Sustainable Values, based on the New Zealand Business Council for Sustainable Development Code of Conduct, as well as a 'sustainability performance review' to be completed over the coming year. Sustainability considerations are built into 'Request for Proposals' and supplier contracts. In December 2006, Green Insurer presented its sustainability category Supplier Award to Corporate Express for the way it had embraced Green Insurer's sustainability policies in delivering its service. Corporate Express scored points for their contribution to Green Insurer's 'Easy Being Green' employee offer, its environmental reporting practices, including disposal of packaging, and its research and consultation on environmentally friendly product alternatives.

However, notwithstanding the public statements in Green Insurer's sustainability report on supplier reporting, internal respondents did not believe that supplier reports were carefully or rigorously checked. Supplier reports were viewed more as a 'boundary report' than a footprint because the reports did not detail the sustainability activities of suppliers. The manager of analytics and reporting described the struggle to coordinate the information gathered in supplier reports:

> First of all we had to arrange with our suppliers an understanding and appreciation of sustainability. So I worked with our category managers at procurement to get agreements from each of our suppliers to say that sustainability is now a core component of your measurement system, to see whether you're a good or bad supplier. So we got a balanced scorecard with our suppliers set up that has things like price, service, timeliness and delivery of goods and that. We also had a section called sustainability. The procurement manager came in around that time and instigated the balanced scorecard with suppliers ... it was a rocky beginning. I had to send some stern letters to them saying if you want to continue with our contract, we do consider this very, very important and that, although it's new and you're probably not getting it from any other customers, we consider ourselves leading in this field and that this is a requirement with us.

Furthermore, there appeared to be a lack of rigorous scrutiny of the underlying data in supplier reports. The manager of analytics and reporting made the following observation:

> Internally I haven't done anything essentially. Our quality check is the point where we receive the data from the supplier. We'll do a quick check there. We've got our category managers informed. It's their responsibility to make sure that the data is looking correct. They're essentially the coalface; they know what's happening with their particular category. And when we, for example, do the annual reports, we get them to sign off the information that's given to us. We do a double check on the assumptions because sometimes the suppliers change assumptions without informing you. Somebody will double check there. If we find discrepancies we ask them to go back and redo it.

While several respondents believed Green Insurer was making significant progress with the collection of sustainability data, in some instances there appeared to be significant problems with underlying data integrity and assurance; and more broadly with the integration of sustainability information for internal decision-making. We now turn to these issues.

SECTION TWO

Sustainability: data collection, measurement and reporting

Several respondents indicated that Green Insurer has a broad range of accounting systems to collect sustainability data. For instance, the organisation has the 'benefits tracker' system for procurement data that was expanded to include CO_2 initiatives. The manager of analytics andreporting stated:

> So, for example, if we did something that led to a cost saving, that would also be reflected as a CO_2 saving. We haven't got anything populating there yet, but the theory is that we get that and report that to the group, just to say these initiatives led to this cost saving plus the CO_2 saving.

Other systems used by Green Insurer internally included SAP-HR and SAP Payroll, SABA (a learning management system) and ARIBA for procurement. One system that got significant mention from respondents in relation to sustainability data collection was the BudgetMaster system. This is a monthly financial system which was expanded by the organisation to collect sustainability information (with the addition of 'Green Dimensions Database'). One surprising aspect of the discussion with respondents was that while there was much discussion around the measurement and collection of data on environmental impacts, there was little or no mention from respondents about the use and effectiveness of environmental management systems. It appeared that Green Insurer did not use such systems. It is not altogether surprising that many respondents noted the lack of integration of sustainability data with internal accounting systems, particularly in terms of producing simple and understandable outputs. The group head of sustainable business practices stated: 'We've got this massive database that's run out of the chief financial office, a system called BudgetMaster. All the data's crunched in there and it's all verified and it's all endlessly complicated.'

The manager of analytics and reporting also noted a lack of centralised approach to management accounting systems within the organisation:

> I think we've never had a central management function ourselves in people. It's been done in each of the areas – CFO doing their own, other operation divisions were doing their own. The only area that will sort of centralise is culture and reputation, but they're more focused on the communication rather than the actual management of it. So we don't have any form of centralised management of it, which is why we don't have a management database for the group on it. Probably pockets of areas of the company have got it.

Green Insurer's consultant for corporate social responsibility stated that timing of the data and the breadth of the information collected were major obstacles for the integration financial information with sustainability data:

> We would like to see the reports integrated. We have some issues around that, one being the timing. Timing is a big issue, and timing is very tight between the end of financial year and the release of an annual report. And the breadth of information that we collect for the sustainability report, the obvious one is electricity. There's always a lag, which is why this year we moved our reporting from June to July to May to June, so that we could actually get that month in earlier so that we could include it in the annual report. But timing is a problem. The other issue for us, or has been until recently,

> is we have a huge shareholder listing, over one million shareholders and, until last year, we didn't have an electronic register of those shareholders. So a lot of our shareholders have now agreed to receive information electronically but most of our shareholders are of a very higher age bracket and they want hard-copies. So the financial cost of effectively doubling the size of the annual report and then releasing it is significant. So my inclination is that the report should be combined, it makes sense that you're seeing one aspect as important as the other – but the reality of making it happen is difficult.

Furthermore, many respondents noted that Green Insurer's international operations significantly complicated the process of integration and presented particular problems for data quality. Green Insurer's consultant for corporate social responsibility stated that 'nervousness' about data quality was a major obstacle to external reporting:

> You know, we know that they have the same systems in Asia but we're not sure of everything that goes in there ... we're not sure of the quality of what's going in and what's coming out. And we're nervous about it ... so group risk assurance will do a lot of work with them before we actually go out publicly.

The lack of integration across the organisation's systems and processes was felt at the division level (such as through human resources). The manager of workforce reporting and analysis, culture and reputation observed the lack of coordination within the group when it came to the balanced scorecard:

> As far as a balanced scorecard, no there isn't that coordination at other levels that I know of. It tends to be we'll provide

HR information and it might get integrated elsewhere. But, yes, we do provide information to what we understand are balanced scorecards. To answer your question about what goes in there, who decides it and what I think is done with it, I think it is very, very poorly understood and very poorly coordinated. My team has historically been very reactive and, in fact, even as little as a year ago were seen and actually did just produce lumps of data; they would just extract data. They are doing a lot more high level reporting now, but even that is reactive, straight reporting and there's not a lot of forecasting. There's not a lot of analysis that goes in there. They would like to do more.

A perhaps more fundamental problem preventing the effective integration of financial and sustainability oriented data is that the organisation had not decided on the type of sustainability information to collect and report. Conspicuous in the interviews with respondents was that the organisation did not publish lead indicators in the sustainability report, such as sustainability targets. Arguably, the sustainability report has value in a decision-making sense because it is a more forward-looking document than financial statements, which rely on largely historical data. However, without lead indicators, the usefulness of the sustainability report can be significant reduced. For instance, when Green Insurer reported on CO_2 emissions the company's sustainability report only compared emissions to last year's emission levels. While this is useful for determining whether emissions behaviour is changing, it is not a target per se, which can drive policy and influence behaviour.

It was evident from the interviews with respondents that Green Insurer had previously experimented with publishing numerous sustainability targets, but had recently gone to the other extreme of publishing few or no targets for external reporting purposes. Green Insurer's consultant for corporate social responsibility stated:

> Yes and when you look at the narrative of the report, we're very up front in saying that previously we had set ridiculous targets that we were never going to meet. And last year we set no targets at all. In the last 12 months we really concentrated on target setting and what those targets would be, particularly around environmental performance ... the annual report details a lot of our people targets as well. But what we've done with our environmental targets is take a back-to-basics approach [to] the biggest influence and impact areas for each division, and we've assigned divisional targets which is then rolled up into an overall corporate target, which is a reduction of three per cent in CO_2 per full time employee.

Another interviewee observed that sustainability targets were merely 'aspirational' and did not reach or impact on the organisation's cost centres. There was some conviction among respondents that targets need to be specified and incentivised within the organisational structure in order to change culture and influence behaviour. For instance, the manager of analytics and reporting remarked that targets should be linked to remuneration to motivate behaviour, stating:

> All I know is that there are some aspirational targets, but it's not made real to cost centre managers because they don't have the direct target themselves, and they don't have something yet, that's linked up to their bonuses. There's no better way of changing people's behaviour than linking it up to a bonus. We've used that for other things in order to get some sustainability initiatives out, and it has shown great success. You back that with the education and give them

the resources, some thinking space on how to do things and they'll become their own champions.

Data integrity

Several respondents mentioned some concerns with the integrity of sustainability information collected within the organisation. The manager of workforce reporting and analysis, culture and reputation stated:

> But at the moment really we know we have problems with data integrity, but we have a bigger problem with perception of data integrity and get involved in a lot of discussions and a lot of justification over the figures we produce, which sometimes are inaccurate. Sometimes that's because of the data and sometimes it's because of our manual reporting systems and somebody in my team is doing something different to somebody else in the team.

For instance, interviews with respondents suggest that turnover data collected by the organisation is little more than a headcount. The systems do not measure, or are not designed to measure the cost invested in an employee (such as training and development costs). Respondents acknowledged there is some complexity in measuring such data reliably. Another problem facing data integrity are lags in the collection and reporting of some types of sustainability data. The manager of workforce, reporting and analysis, culture and reputation stated:

> Because of the audit, one of the big problems which we have in the HR data is late reporting of changes. Now again, I am not a finance person, but I tend to understand that in finance it's much more controlled because of the legal implications on it. But yeah you don't just put a payment back and say

backdate this to last year ... I mean some terminations tend
to be a little bit late; safety data is particularly poor. You tend
to find that two weeks after you've closed off the measure, it's
a lot different.

The acting senior manager of group risk assurance also raised
major concerns about the integrity of the data, stating:

From a BudgetMaster point of view, BudgetMaster as I'm sure
you know, has been developed to be a sustainability reporting
tool and for last year's indicator exercise, we did actually ask,
if you have the environmental data in BudgetMaster, give me
the data. Let's go through it, through the correct channel. The
integrity of that data was shocking.

The questionable reliability of data may explain why senior
managers are reluctant to report sustainability information externally
or integrate the information into actual economic decision-making.
The senior manager, sustainable business practices stated:

Well, but also just in terms of the NGERS [National
Greenhouse and Energy Reporting System], I mean our
CFO, when we issued our first report ... he was having heart
failure saying, 'I am not releasing any data unless I'm 100 per
cent sure it's going to be right, and it's the right stuff'. And I
don't blame him for that.

On a positive note, several respondents indicated that data capture
was improving in the organisation. Green Insurer's consultant for
corporate social responsibility stated:

They've [the company] been quick to improve. Previously I
worked for a government organisation that was producing
sustainability reports and that was a challenge because

they were slow to improve the systems because there wasn't seen to be value in improving systems. Whereas for a big corporate organisation that needs to move quickly, that's hungry and has an appetite for growth internationally as well as domestically, our systems really have to keep up. And that's been fantastic as far as the sustainability report goes. I mean, of course there are always areas that are weak and I've never worked in an organisation that hasn't found headcount a difficult figure to find, which seems just the most ridiculous thing in the world, but we're at a stage now where we're very confident in the systems that sit behind us and our feedback from our auditor has consistently been, since that first report, that our systems are now at a very good stage.

It was also clear from respondents that the organisation was progressing with the integration of some forms of sustainability data. For instance, the procurement manager stated:

> We do capture the information through the financial system so, to use paper as an example, we would have various methodologies of capturing information around that and that's obviously financial dollars spent just going through your normal general ledger processing invoices and the like ... we have interfaces with the suppliers where they provide volume information, which is then uploaded into our reporting systems. And ultimately that then flows firstly to our capture systems like SAP and then flows through into our reporting systems in BudgetMaster. It would be in those reporting systems where we're actually doing our allocation around a conversion to CO_2 equivalent.

Is sustainability information actually used for decision-making?

It was clear from several respondents that sustainability information was often included in monthly budgets and reports. According to some respondents, all cost centre managers had access to monthly reporting on the environmental performance, although the information was relatively limited. The consultant for corporate social responsibility stated:

> Of course they have access to most of our financial figures but some of our people figures are things like turnover and absenteeism. They don't have monthly access to things like women in senior management, mainly because that's something that we would only calculate on a 12-monthly basis; there's no real monthly value in including that. The only other indicator, environmental indicator, that's not included in the cost centre managers' reports, is electricity consumption. And that's because they have no control over that at an individual level. That's determined by property and asset management, which is within our CFO area so they have that [electricity reduction] as one of their corporate targets.

Respondents also indicated that senior management and executives received monthly reports on Green Insurer's sustainability performance, which covered the spectrum of safety, workplace, environmental and financial performance. However, notwithstanding that sustainability information appeared to be made available to cost centres and divisional managers, it was clear from many respondents that sustainability information did not impact the internal decision-making process of the business in a significant way. The consultant for corporate social responsibility stated:

> If you spoke to every cost centre manager in the organisation
> they'd say to you, 'No, I don't look at environmental reporting'.
> Some of them would, some of them wouldn't but that's still
> part of the cultural process, as well as the reporting.

Other data worth considering with regards to decision-making is employee and workforce data. However, the manager of workforce reporting and analysis, culture and reputation suggested that employee and workforce data may not be widely used within the organisation for decision-making:

> We're trying to provide turnover and absenteeism figures,
> I think environment is still struggling, I perceive, to just
> provide those basic CO_2 usage, paper usage, and it's very
> much the same. And they don't get much attention either.
> It gets reported, some areas take it seriously, some areas try
> and do what they can. But I think in the end most people in
> the company are probably still not quite engaging with the
> concept that we do this because we're an insurance company
> and because it's not the impact we have, it's the fact that
> we're trying to lead this in the business world. I think people
> understand it, I just don't think that they engage with that
> concept.

The consultant for corporate social responsibility stated that sustainability information was only used in a limited capacity because it was not embedded into the performance targets of individual executives:

> The thing is with sustainability, we manage a lot of the
> cultural side and a lot of the reporting, it's very clear to all of
> our executives that they each individually have responsibility
> for ensuring that sustainability is part of their performance.

In terms of whether sustainability is having an impact, the group chief financial officer saw traditional financial metrics as having the most clout, and raised concerns about mixing the financial and sustainability metrics, stating:

> ROE [return on equity] and more traditional drivers is what we get asked questions about. These things are – if you wanted to pursue a discussion with any of the fund managers about this issue [sustainability], they're all very well versed and they can talk to you for ages on it very authoritatively and they can quote all the research. Do they actually use it to drive their decision-making? I'm not aware of anyone that does that, no ... and we want to be influential in the decision-making around this stuff. That's fine. I don't have a problem with that. But ... as far as the role goes going forward with how it fits with our reporting, I don't like mixing oil and water. I'm an accountant. It's just the way I am and I'd rather not incorporate it into the annual report until we understand exactly what's required. But I'd also like us to be very well prepared and work a lot more on embedding it in our culture and our business units in the interim.

While many respondents suggested that sustainability information was not widely used in internal decision-making, sustainability information was perceived to assume an important 'public relations' role. For instance, the consultant for corporate social responsibility stated that the sustainability report is always taken to the analyst briefings and annual general meeting (AGM) because it is a forward-looking document, whereas financial information is largely historical:

> As part of our AGM and as part of our analyst briefings that we do, the CEO always brings the sustainability report

and talks about a sustainability performance and the group executive, culture and reputation is always saying that if you want a future-looking document look at our sustainability report because annual reports are always looking [backwards] whereas this is actually telling you where a company is going. If you want to know if a company is going to do well, have a look at their engagement scores. If you want to know if a company is not doing well, have a look at their turnover scores.

According to several respondents, in order to make sustainability information more useful to the organisation, targets need to be formally established and managers incentivised around these targets. The consultant for corporate social responsibility stated:

We don't have, at an individual level, targets tied to performance around environmental sustainable performance consistently. Some areas are really great at doing that, some areas aren't paying as much attention to that, but this year the CEO has set sustainability targets for all the executives so I'm thinking that next year their people will be more interested in what we're doing around sustainability.

The manager of analytics and reporting stated:

My understanding is that I find it hard that people are changing behaviours unless they have a target. There's a small portion of people, they are changing behaviours because they look beyond the targets. They see that this is important. But I couldn't say that's the general mass of people.

The group head of sustainable business practices observed:

We have internal targets. The question is about when they become public. It's not that they don't exist. I mean, we don't manage our performance in a vacuum. It's the question around being more public about them.

He also stated 'And yes, we can report on this stuff, but we're still missing some of the basics ... incentivising people to those targets.'

Combining financial and sustainability reports

At the time of the interviews, Green Insurer did not combine the sustainability report with the annual report. Some respondents noted that separating the two reports creates the impression that the sustainability report is the 'poorer cousin' of the annual report. The head of group treasury and finance seemed to reflect the view of many respondents that the reports should be combined, stating:

> The annual reports are so fat, what's a little bit more on it. I think it would be positive to do that. I think the sustainability report often just becomes sort of the 'poor cousin' and the focus is on the shareholders and the financials and then the sustainability report goes out and it's probably not anywhere near as widely read.

The group head of sustainable business practices stated that combining the reports was highly desirable, but also identified significant dilemmas that might face the organisation if the two reports were combined, one being the potential ramifications of a qualified audit report:

> The other thing we're trying to do, but not lose the extent of information that we already report on, is to ... crunch together our sustainability reporting into our annual report. In terms of reach, we're straight up. It would improve massively, because we have a million shareholders. So that's one reason. But the other reason is around our strong view ... that lead indicators are far more valuable indicators of the

health of a company than lag indicators. It's very complicated, in terms of audit requirements, because even something that's perfectly reasonable, but a bit peculiar, relative to the accounting standard, as you talk about, can give you a qualified audit. So that just sends our CFO into outer orbit. I mean, you know, that's the last thing a corporation can allow itself is a qualified audit, even if it's for perfectly explainable reasons. Doesn't matter. That terminology makes CFOs pass out, not to mention shareholders.

On the other hand, including the sustainability report in a few pages of the annual report (and allowing details to be searched online) has been viewed as a positive step by the organisation. The consultant for corporate social responsibility stated:

The feedback we had from last year's concise report, which is the first year we did it, was overwhelming. [People said,] 'Please keep doing it, we don't want to see a long printed version, keep the long information on the website so that we can search around it'.

But overwhelmingly people were very keen to see the report produced in a concise format.

Assurance

Respondents indicated that Green Insurer takes the sustainability assurance process seriously, but it has been a steep learning curve. The consultant for corporate social responsibility stated:

Yes, we very much looked at external auditors to give us some guidance on the rigour of our data ... there was a lovely idea before I joined the organisation that we'll just release the sustainability report and let's get (the auditor) in to have a look at the figures and we'll just release them in the next couple of weeks, kind of thing. [The auditor] looked at the figures and went, 'Wow, you guys have no idea what you're doing. You really need to start back at basics and look at what your systems are, what your controls are and start from scratch.

Respondents indicated that Green Insurer would not necessarily be targeting a higher level of assurance accreditation under G3. As stated by the consultant for corporate social responsibility:

Assurance is a bit of a bugbear for us, and I think because of that general disconnect. I mean, it's still early days for Green Insurer. This is only our third sustainability report. When we looked at doing the first sustainability report, I was very keen to tender and I wanted to select a variety of people to show us the kind of verification we could have and our CFO was very concerned about that and didn't want us to move away from our traditional audit partner which is why we have the auditor.

However, respondents noted there has been a shift away from the auditor to using a different assurance provider. There are a few possible explanations for this. First, one respondent noted the implications outlined in the *Sarbanes-Oxley Act 2002* about using the same audit firm for non-audit-related services. The consultant for corporate social responsibility observed:

Now, no one actually picked up that some of those non-audit fees are in fact the assurance statement for the sustainability report. But the shareholder raised that issue of, you know, do you realise that this is against the Sarbanes-Oxley and, if you're ever wanting to expand to America, how would you deal with this because that would mean that you couldn't expand to America. And he's absolutely right, which is why a lot of companies like Westpac and the like use a variety of assurance providers rather than just the one.

Another problem identified by respondents is that a Big Four firm does not add significant value to the assurance process. The manager, analytics and reporting stated:

> You can only do so much with an audit. They do what they're programmed to do which is to look at the processes. Are there any risky areas there? If there are, look into it, and if there's not ... we're very, very picky about our documentation. So we've got everything documented from day one. I heard from the auditors that's the best they've seen so we're very happy with that.

The manager of group statutory reporting and consolidation stated that cost was a key driver in moving to another assurance provider:

> There were a number of things attached to it. I'm on the panel to do the selection. One thing is when we looked at the original cost by the Big Four it's very expensive ... we started to question whether it was worth it. The second thing is other than the verification work, did they add any value to our practices or to what we're trying to achieve going forward? By looking at these main two areas at the moment we didn't feel our old service provider actually gave us both.

SECTION THREE

Stakeholder engagement

Green Insurer's 2006–07 sustainability report identified several potential stakeholder groups for sustainability information, including: customers, shareholders, employees, government bodies and regulators, suppliers, unions, community partners, business organisations and industry groups. However, it was clear from many respondents that stakeholders were not extensively engaged in the collection and reporting of sustainability information within the organisation.

There was debate among some respondents on how the term 'stakeholder' should even be defined. The consultant for corporate social responsibility stated:

> We're an organisation that has an incredible reach. So when you're talking about our stakeholders, we need to define exactly who key stakeholders are. We've advised that they liaise with our executive who will give them a suggested list of stakeholders. And those stakeholders are both people who we would be happy for them to talk to and people that we recognise as key stakeholders who we simply wouldn't like them not to speak to.

Some respondents did not perceive external stakeholders to be the focus of their sustainability reporting. The manager of workforce reporting and analysis, culture and reputation stated that 'our concentration is very much with the internal stakeholders'. The group head of sustainable business practices stated:

> The single biggest strategic question for us – and it's the one that exercises the mind of our Expert Community Advisory

> Committee, you know we have a committee set up of
> independent advisers – is how we choose them [stakeholders]
> and who gets to play a role in choosing them.

The group chief financial officer stated there was very little feedback from stakeholders in the context of Green Insurer's sustainability reporting. 'In the ten years I've been in this role, I've had questions from one investor based in Melbourne on one occasion. That's it.'

In terms of whether the supply chain sustainability policies have any impact on stakeholder engagement, the consultant for corporate social responsibility stated:

> I can tell you the only case that I've heard recently, the only
> case, that's as far as my knowledge extends, we've ever had
> from our commercial customers on our supply chain and
> how we manage our sustainability was around community
> engagement, who were we involved with? And they decided
> to go with us rather than the other commercial insurance
> provider because we did have a relationship with the
> Salvation Army. It's the only example we've ever heard.

SECTION FOUR

Hurdles facing the collection, integration and reporting of sustainability information

Respondents in Green Insurer identified several hurdles facing the efficient and effective collection and integration of sustainability information within the organisation. The most significant obstacle identified by respondents related to corporate culture and education, particularly achieving senior executive buy in. Other concerns related to some cynicism about the value of sustainability information and the lack of coordination on sustainability initiatives across the organisation.

Corporate culture and resistance

The manager of analytics and reporting observed that a major factor behind corporate resistance to sustainability in the organisation was a lack of understanding of the basic concept of sustainability and what it means in a practical sense to the business, stating:

> There ha[s] been resistance ... around the place. I think it's only because of the way it was approached at the start. I think something like it's conceptually very new ... as laypeople you don't understand what it's about. All you know is it's something to do with the environment, and there have been plenty of thoughts in the past about hippies or whatever. A lot of people will bring up those images in their mind. This is something silly or crazy ... I think one of the major lessons I got out of it, if I was to apply it in the future anywhere else, is there's a certain approach in educating people about this. You can't tell people to do it. You can't tell people to believe it overnight. You have to convince them about it and get them owning it.

Another resistance point is convincing senior managers in a profit-driven culture that sustainability actually adds value to the organisation. In response to a question about whether sustainability provides a competitive advantage, the group head of sustainable business practices said:

> We get that argument all the time [that it does not provide a competitive advantage]. I just gave a major address to Macquarie on Monday and I got hammered around that. They said, 'well there you are ... there are only three Australian companies who are in the global 100 sustainability companies of the world'. They said, 'Look at you guys. You've got consistent profitability, but not stellar'.

The group head of sustainable business practices discussed major difficulties in convincing accountants about the benefit of sustainability:

> Jobs like mine are really, really bruising. The first trajectory is that heads of sustainability fight with the CFO for at least two years, which I did, like everyone else who has my job. He's kind of turned around. In fact, he's our biggest champion, now, on energy efficiency and he's wanting to invest in wind turbines. I mean, he's incredible. He's completely turned around. Now, I've got the hard heads who run the businesses to convince. It's a constant change management work in progress ... it's totally financially driven. CFOs don't think about anything other than finance. Absolutely utterly financial.

The senior manager, sustainable business practices added:

> It's very hard to get it through the company ... I was very disappointed, you've got to go through these fights four or five times before they hear you. We had a guy approach us

who wanted to undertake a forestry sequestration insurance product and our actuaries weren't great [supporters of the idea] ... so it didn't get up. But that's exactly it, give it a couple of years and you know, it was a classic discussion around short-termism versus long-termism. So we [my boss and I] had this fight on the phone about what he was on about, the numbers just don't stack up and I said, 'Yeah, well, have you built into your business case the fact that this is a potential product that could be quite substantial in 2010?' And he was like, 'Well, we've got no expertise,' and I said, 'Well, no one has got expertise'.

The acting senior manager of group risk assurance stated that senior executive buy-in with regards to sustainability was a major problem in the beginning, but that the culture had improved within the organisation. He said:

Honestly, I don't think there was senior executive buy-in, which is one of the key problems. You had a couple of the key players absolutely extolling the virtues of sustainability, however the rest of the executive team [said], 'I'm not wasting my time on that. What's that going to do from a commercial point of view? That's not going to help me'. I don't think the link between sustainability – and this goes back to the whole being green thing – and the commercial advantages of it had actually been made. It's really taken some time for them to build that up and that's a real stumbling block to anything else.

Sustainability is resource-intensive

Another issue raised by respondents is that collecting and reporting sustainability data is a very resource-intensive exercise.

The chief risk officer and group actuary stated that a major hurdle facing the sustainability culture was the perceived cost of sustainability and not the underlying philosophy:

> The usual brick wall is they [companies] don't want to pay the money to put in a system or collect another piece of data. I mean, that's the inevitable. That's the usual brick wall ... so we haven't really had too many brick walls in this organisation on ideas and philosophy I'd have to say, but I mean that's certainly a lot to do with key people in place. I think also ... it became evident from our employee staff surveys that this really was something that helped motivate staff and particularly helped us recruit younger people. There's no doubt about that at all. It definitely does help.

The manager of workforce reporting and analysis, culture and reputation stated:

> I think it's [putting a value on sustainability] a solution so we can engage with accountants and managers. However, although it's a very valuable thing to do, it is also something that's very resource-intensive. It takes a long time to put values on and it means that you take away from the limited work that we're already resourced to do.

The group head of sustainable business practices had the following observations about the resources required in reporting sustainability:

> Our sustainability report is becoming a huge job, because we have to crunch data from all over the world. So it's hard enough getting all of the GRI indicators from the Australian businesses ... and this is without the Asian and UK people – we have 80 individual indicator owners that need to be

liaised with ... it's an incredibly complicated exercise, if you do it properly.

The acting senior manager of group risk assurance made the point that once executives understood that sustainability was good for the bottom line, the culture was quick to change:

> The steps, I think, were really taken while the business was making that connection [between sustainability and a reduction on the bottom line]. Sustainability is not just about being green, sustainability is about a lot more things. It's actually about how we work in our day-to-day work environment; it's about what we do in the community and it's actually then been linked back to our products. It's actually making it a tangible kind of thing. For example, it's all about risk reduction for us. It actually makes sense for us to help the community out there to stop burglaries, because that means we get less claims, which means that our premiums become cheaper and everybody's happy. And it's making that link through for people to actually go, 'Oh, this actually does have an impact, this actually can affect us from a commercial point of view' ... I think all of a sudden, those sceptics have actually gone, 'Oh, there actually might be something to this'.

Lack of collaboration/integration

Several respondents observed that the lack of coordination, integration and collaboration in the collection and reporting of sustainability data across the organisation was a major obstacle in forming sustainability initiatives. For instance, the sustainability manager within one of the divisions lamented the lack of collaboration on sustainability issues and the 'silo effect' across the group, saying:

I think it's probably fair to say that aside from the reporting process and aside from the climate change work that we try and leverage at a [divisional] level, there is very little collaboration ... we are now doing an awful lot in the business, so I want to really try and drive that through. Because it is good for the business, it's good for the team, it's great for me, I'm learning bucket loads.

The manager of workforce reporting and analysis, culture and reputation observed that, 'when areas are split, the silos develop sometimes more than others, depending on who's managing it and what they do about the teamwork'.

Another respondent noted that there were no definitive reporting obligations to provide sustainability information across the group. The consultant for corporate social responsibility stated:

One of the difficulties is that I deal with probably 80 indicator owners, so primary and secondary contacts for all our indicator owners. And none of those have any requirements to give me any information. They have no kind of formal requirements in their job to be nice to me, so that's very much around relationship-building.

Some respondents indicated that things could improve in promoting a better sustainability culture at Green Insurer. When questioned about what could be done differently, the manager, analytics and reporting stated:

First of all I would form a team centrally that would have the responsibility and accountability of making this happen and work. I would then go through top-down, the list of the top 100 people and pinpoint which ones we needed as stakeholders to be engaged. Then I would have a chat to them about it, socialise some of the ideas, figure out what will work for them, what motivates them, develop plans around that, get them on board. Then educate them that this isn't just a 'greenie' thing; this is an economical thing for the company. Then concurrently I'd be working on what I did with the data and the reporting. I would then get a first cut of that, analyse it and determine [that], okay we need to take a step forward and set some targets. Whether they're right or wrong, let's set some targets without linking it to bonuses in the first year. Then we'd see how that goes. We'd get two years of experience under our belts and then we're in a much better position to set some targets. At the same time, within those two years, you'd start the education process to a greater mass of people out there. You'd do it through the central function as well as using your stakeholders. At that time they'd become the champions, and you'd roll those out.

Several respondents noted that sustainability targets needed to be directly linked to bonuses to incentivise staff. For instance, the consultant for corporate social responsibility stated:

That's part of the kind of cultural communications program that we do. Yes, so a lot of our internal communications is around that but we also work with our remuneration team around bonuses, and group executive, culture and reputation, at their level, works with the CEO to determine bonuses. We've certainly found previously that when we had an all staff target around safety, safety improved dramatically ... and we're finding areas that are a problem, like turnover, which is a problem for us this year, and last year, will be directly tied to people's remuneration. Money talks unfortunately.

The manager of innovation and sustainability stated:

> Well, it's certainly part of what we consider is sustainability in
> Green Insurer. In the CFO's Sustainability Committee, we're
> conscious to always make sure that sustainability isn't just
> about the environmental side of it. Having said that, that's
> the area where we're probably most lacking and need to do
> the most work and support Green Insurer the most, so we do
> a lot in that space. But safety is another aspect and, say, last
> year, one of our targets for the division – and we had one per
> cent of everyone's bonus tied to this – was introducing safety
> initiatives for CFO, which CFO Sustainability Committee
> ended up doing.

A case study analysis of Herbal Life

Background of Herbal Life

Herbal Life is an ASX 300 listed company and one of Australia's leading natural health brands. The company operates in Australia, New Zealand and Asia and currently employs more than 400 people in the region. The company provides a wide spectrum of vitamin and dietary supplements covering children's health; cold, flu and immunity; digestive health; energy; everyday health; eye health; heart and circulation; men's health; nails; hair and skin nutritional oils; stress relief; weight management; and women's health.

The company claims that its products are developed using a combination of scientific evidence and 'hundreds of years of traditional knowledge'. Further, the company states that its products are made to the exacting requirements of the international PIC/S standards of Good Manufacturing Practice. The company also claims to use high quality ingredients for its products sourced from around the world. The company's annual report 2007 stated: 'Our product formulations are approved by regulatory bodies where they are sold and are required to meet both our own and various governments' stringent standards of safety, quality and efficacy.'

In terms of business operations, Herbal Life is primarily a marketing and packaging company – it does not manufacture its own products. The director R&D and corporate affairs stated:

> As a manufacturer, we're basically a marketing office. So onsite, because we don't make anything, we just pack stuff into bottles, we're not a great user of water or energy. We're not a great polluter.

Herbal Life has a different profile from the other case organisations studied. As a small ASX company, Herbal Life does not have a strong analyst following and is a relatively illiquid stock. The chief financial officer stated: 'Herbal Life is quite unique. By market capital, we would be in the top 300, but by liquidity we don't get anywhere near ASX 300.'

The chief financial officer also observed that Herbal Life was more akin to a family company, given its size and culture, but the company has been rapidly expanding of late:

> If there was a spectrum, we'd be definitely on the family company end of it. However, we've grown. I mean, I think three or four years ago when I started, our sales were about $100 million and they're now $170 million, so we've had 70 per cent growth in three or four years. And it hasn't been through 'raping and pillaging', I can tell you. You say there are some benefits from doing all this and having it embedded in the culture. I believe a lot of people buy our products because they know that we're a good company. We treat our staff well and they're getting a good quality product. We're not cheap. We're the premium product but people are willing to pay for that. And I think that is proof that the people definitely do buy on that basis. It's a point of differentiation, it really is.

The company also has a strong reputation in the industry for superior financial performance and product innovation. At the time of the interviews, Herbal Life achieved a record profit for the financial year, with strong increases in sales (up 4.2 per cent to $178.8 million). Herbal Life's international business also grew 1.8 per cent in that year. In addition to the launch of seven new products in the 2007 financial year, Herbal Life achieved substantial market share growth across the stress and pregnancy segments, with continued success from joint formula within the arthritis, joint, bone and muscle category. Innovative product communications and positioning helped influence the preference of the brand. Herbal Life's financial results and reputation for leadership and innovation were recognised through a number of awards, including the 2007 Best Managed Company in Australia (small cap corporate of the year) by *Asia Money Magazine.*

Regulatory environment of Herbal Life

Herbal Life is a public company governed by various Corporations Act and ASX listing rules. In addition, Herbal Life's products are made to exacting requirements under the international PIC/S (Pharmaceutical Inspection Convention and Pharmaceutical Inspection Co-operation Scheme) standards of good manufacturing practice. Herbal Life's product formulations are approved by regulatory bodies where they are sold and are required to meet both Australian and various other governments' standards of safety, quality and efficacy.

Why Herbal Life was selected for a case study

Herbal Life was selected as a case study given its established corporate reputation as a leader in the sustainability field. In his interview with the researchers, the chairman of the board noted the close and natural affinities between the success of a leading natural healthcare brand and principles of sustainability, stating:

> Herbal Life has had a long history of being involved in environmental issues. Because we deal with nature, we deal with natural products, we have a philosophical underpinning of the company that aligns us with. In fact, let me put it to you this way. If Herbal Life dirtied the environment it would be far worse for us than if Shell did or a cigarette company did or somebody like that. So there's an inherent need for us to be mindful of things about which we may not necessarily have product but we have to be mindful of.

Herbal Life was also selected because it is a public company that is expected to report to established stakeholder groups on sustainability. An interesting feature of Herbal Life is that while it is a public company with strong commitments to sustainability and the environment, it does not prepare a separate sustainability report, nor do many of its initiatives appear to be widely promoted or publicised to key stakeholder groups. A commitment to sustainability appears to be deeply inculcated internally within the culture of the organisation, but not aggressively promoted outside the organisation.

Overview of the case study

This case analysis is organised as follows:

Section one explores some of the issues surrounding the public image of sustainability projected by Herbal Life and the perceptions of sustainability reporting by respondents working daily with the programs and initiatives within the organisation.

Section two explores Herbal Life's processes, systems and methodologies for the collection, integration and reporting of sustainability information.

Section three explores the extent to which stakeholder engagement influences or impacts on sustainability reporting practices within the organisation.

Section four discusses potential hurdles confronting the collection, integration and reporting of sustainability information with the organisation.

Finally, some conclusions and policy implications are considered.

SECTION ONE

Public image versus internal perceptions

The key sustainability initiatives of Herbal Life are substantial and appear to be deeply embedded in the culture of the organisation. The interviews suggest that Herbal Life is different from other respondents in that the company seemingly does not promote itself very aggressively or assertively as a leader in sustainability, nor does the company collect and report much sustainability information, either externally or internally. The company appears to practice a culture of sustainability without need for comprehensive formal measurements and reporting.

Herbal Life's commitment to sustainability is evidenced by a number of internal initiatives within the organisation. At the time of the interviews, the company was in the process of developing a new purpose-built head office and manufacturing and distribution facility. This 'new generation' workspace has been designed to have minimal impact on the environment. Among other things, the complex will harvest its own rainwater, and will possess its own electricity generation plant. The company claims that the complex will be the first tri-generation plant of its type in Australia and one of a few in the world where all waste heat from the plant engines are fully utilised, providing a hot and cold water service, space heating and lap pool heating. According to the company, the plant is expected to save about 2300 tonnes of CO_2 emissions per annum (which is equivalent to taking about 1000 cars off the road).

Herbal Life has fostered a sustainability culture with its employees. For instance, several of the interview respondents observed that Herbal Life was particularly committed to the welfare and development of its employees. For instance, from its annual report it can be seen that the new complex at Warriewood was designed to encompass facilities to help employees achieve 'optimum wellness and maintain a healthy work–life balance', and includes a gym, swimming pool and massage centre. Herbal Life also promotes the development of staff through various training courses and programs to encourage 'superior performance, higher levels of engagement and expansion of the leadership pool'. The company invested in a senior development program to inspire strong leadership and best business practice. Many respondents indicated that Herbal Life was dedicated to providing a family-friendly and supportive workplace for employees. This was reflected in the implementation of a 'Stop Smoking' campaign within the organisation, based on behavioural change and hypnotherapy. The company also has an Employee Assistance Program, which was introduced to provide support for employees experiencing personal problems.

Among other initiatives, Herbal Life participates in the National Packaging Covenant (NPC) which was frequently mentioned by respondents. The NPC aims to achieve improvement in environmental performance of Herbal Life's packaging operations. As a signatory to the NPC since 2001, Herbal Life has been committed to reduce the environmental impact of packaging, close the recycling loop and develop economically viable and sustainable recycling systems. The inclusion of NPC training into Herbal Life's list of official courses, with compulsory attendance for all staff, has led to the company redesigning its packaging to incorporate the recycling logo.

Many respondents noted that the strong sustainability culture of the organisation was inculcated at all levels of the organisation. One of the group's financial accountants said, 'Everyone's very aware of the social and environmental [culture]. I mean with social we actually have employee donations the company will match. So that's very much encouraged as well.' The director R&D and corporate affairs also commented on the organisation's culture, stating:

> It depends on where they [people] are in the company. I think there is some sort of osmosis that happens here, and the number of our suppliers that walk into our foyer for the first time or the staff lounge ... [feel] there is a vibe here. I still get the vibe, whether I'm too close to it or not, I don't know, but it's a nice place to work.

A recurring theme with respondents is that the organisation's success in sustainability can be partly attributed to a lack of fixation on bottom line measures of performance. The group financial controller stated:

> Look, I guess from my perspective, one of the things I like about Herbal Life is that it's not just about the bottom line, because if it was, it wouldn't be the place to work that it is now. So I don't think that's all ... I think there are a number of things that we do and we make decisions which we think in the long-term aren't necessarily cost, maybe are cost neutral, or probably in the long-term better because everyone's happier. I mean, surely if everyone's happy, if everyone's productive, if everyone likes their job, then no one ever leaves. Then you've got a good, dare I use the word 'sustainable', kind of model to have a successful company and at the end of the day that will return itself with good profit as well.

Some of the company's accountants are from non-traditional backgrounds, such as naturopathy. This translates into a lack of fixation on numbers and more tolerance for non-financial indicators of performance. The chief financial officer (CFO) stated:

> I guess for me as well, I'm not a traditional accountant and I don't think many people in my department are. I just think that this is a company that would be very receptive to

recording information that's not necessarily financial. And I just think, to me, culturally, it could be really great for the finance department just to change cultures or to get them involved in things that aren't purely numbers.

One of the corporate financial accountants made the following remark about the CFO: 'He's not as concerned with, you know, having the bottom line spot on ... there is a bit of flexibility there.'

The CFO stated that the cultural focus of the organisation was emphasised when looking for prospective employees:

Yeah absolutely and I just read a great write up, I can't remember it word-for-word, but it's basically saying you can have whatever strategy you want, but if your culture's not right, then you can forget it. I guess this is the point I'm coming to. In Herbal Life, it [the cultural focus] is embedded in our culture. We have very strong values as well, and so if you look at all the stuff we print, it emphasises the strength of values. We do a peer interview here for prospective employees. They'll have the interview with the line manager or whatever, then we do a peer interview with a selection of people across the company to make sure they're going to fit in with the culture of the company. Now that's one thing we do. I've taken it to another level ... when I'm employing someone in finance I'll do a peer interview across functions, but also do a peer interview with the people. Because the hardest thing I find is that, if they don't get on and I've got a turnover of staff every two or three months, it's just a waste of money and a waste of time. They're not productive if they don't get on, so give the people the right to choose.

The company is also a generous donor to several community causes, including Macular Degeneration Foundation, Heart Research

Institute, Herbalife Eye Unit Myanmar (Burma). As mentioned earlier, the company also has a policy of matching staff donations. Staff are encouraged to participate in a charitable scheme whereby 0.5 per cent of their taxable pay is deducted each payday and placed in an interest-bearing trust account. The company matches this and twice yearly each participating employee nominates a registered charity to receive the donation.

SECTION TWO

Sustainability: data collection, measurement and reporting

One of the intriguing features of the Herbal Life sustainability story is the lack of formal collection and analysis of sustainability data within the organisation. This was noted by many respondents. The director of R&D and corporate affairs said, 'I'm not making excuses for the fact that we don't have lots of management systems'.

He also observed that:

> Because most of the stuff that we do downstairs, because we're a therapeutic goods packer, we are inspected by the TGA [Therapeutic Good Administration] and there are certain requirements that we have to fulfil for that which we do. Again, I'm not making excuses, but that drives our immediate environment.

The COO and general manager identified some of the reasons that measurement and reporting was not a strong part of the organisational culture:

> Look, I wouldn't say sustainability reporting per se has been a big ticket item for Herbal Life. It's not that we don't have a lot going on in that area. It's just that it hasn't been one that we've sat there and said, 'oh, we need to improve' and as a result we're measuring this and measuring that. We have some selective projects that we've embarked on like with SEDA [Sustainable Energy Development Authority] and energy and monitoring that ... we've done things like when we wanted to improve our waste water we were monitoring that, but now we've got it down to virtually zero. You know

we don't continually monitor. So I suppose, in that respect, we're not a terrific model for you because I don't have an extensive list of sustainable reporting.

Could we do it? The issue for us as a small organisation is, are we reporting for you or are we reporting for us? And I suppose it's a little bit of a catch 22. Because I got up last year and spoke to the shareholders. I said it was really frustrating that a lot of companies seem to be stealing our space. It's sort of like Herbal Life has had this reputation so linked to the brand around so many different, I suppose, sustainability parameters, whether it be social responsibility or environmental ... so, the difficulty was that without those metrics that were easily comparable, we just stood there and said, 'well we're doing it', so it's a bit of a hard sell in that regard. As far as when we won the Sustainability Award, we've got the information because we had to go back and get it to document for that. But I have to be honest; it's not front and centre all the time.

She also stated:

We'd probably do more around keeping it [sustainability] at the forefront of employee's minds through demonstration of what we're doing, rather than programs to get there. So we would have told them about our lighting project to reduce [energy usage, but] everybody's pretty well focused on the new site at the moment and so we're not doing an awful lot of retro fitting sustainability things around here. The new site, it's absolutely terrific.

In terms of integration and data capture, the chief technology officer stated:

Our ability to capture that information and capture it in a way that we can report on it or analyse it is very limited. I can't think of any systems that we have in place that would allow us to do that. JD Edwards is just purely capturing the financial information around those transactions.

And further:

There are a number of data areas, I guess, available to you in JD Edwards and the problem will be – just depending on what that information is and how you want to use it – if they're numbers it's quite easy to capture. But when they become textual type information, it is very difficult. It's one thing to capture it, but within a JD Edwards system, what you would do with that information, you are very limited on what you could do with that information because it is a standard database-type backend and your data has to be very well defined and clearly defined. When you start getting to textual information, you just don't have that clarity over it so it becomes a bit harder. Secondly, if you look at just a broad range of information just to use the example of the electricity bill, you could have the AP system set up so that some of the fields – and there are literally hundreds of fields within the AP system – you can capture during the entry of an invoice. And some of those are fields you can set however you want. They are actually there as customer-defined fields. But when you set that field that's what that field is for, for every AP invoice. So while you may want to capture kilowatts off a power bill, you may want to capture megalitres off a water bill etc.

The chief technology officer also commented on the lack of formal measurement of sustainability indicators, but believes that more measurement is desirable:

> We're much more about let's get in there and do something other than measure it. Whether – in some of the sustainability stuff we do – that's a measure of the fact of, well, we really don't care, whether that has the ability to increase the EPS [earnings per share] or do something with the share price or do something else, we have a view that's just the right thing to do. So that may be a little bit of a driver. I think having measures and being able to report on them and being able to collate information would be a good thing though. Sometimes you get yourself into a situation where you may be doing things and you may think it's the right thing to do, but unless you can measure what's happened previously and what the benefits were and what the outcome was, how do you know what the things are you should focus on moving forward, because we do have a finite amount of resources.

In terms of sustainability and triple bottom line (TBL) reporting, the corporate communications manager stated:

> I work with finance on the back end of it as well. We did have a conversation a few years ago – I've only got a very top line exposure to it – about triple bottom line reporting and whether or not this was a direction that we wanted to go. At the time it was a decision that we made that even though we think it's really important that we include commentary about social and environmental responsibility, that we actually wouldn't be going as far as triple bottom line reporting and putting dollar figures or accountability or measurements or things like that onto some of the things that we do.

And further:

> Some of it [the data] wasn't actually 'capturable' at the time,
> I suppose if that's a word ... the mechanisms that would need
> to be put in place to make some of the initiatives measurable
> would take an enormous amount of work to get in place. If
> I can give an example: in the National Packaging Covenant,
> now that we have to be a lot more accountable since we've
> actually signed the new covenant, a lot of the things that
> we've been working towards are just getting the systems right
> so that we can measure what we're doing. And it is a lot more
> complex in our business than just simply measuring what
> comes in, what goes out, you know, things like that. So, at the
> time when we did discuss it, it actually wasn't considered to
> be a direction that we would go.

When asked whether accounting systems play much of a role in
the company in terms of environmental issues, the director R&D
and corporate affairs stated:

> Certainly not in the environmental area. It has an input
> in the social and cultural aspects of the business I guess ...
> we've got an executive committee. The head of the finance
> department is on that committee and obviously has an
> influence and a say. So where do I see accounting? If there's a
> cost to be compliant or to be better than compliant in terms
> of minimising the impact of your footprint, is there a point
> where the accounting function would say we can't afford to
> do that?

Even in terms of the NPC, Herbal Life's substantive environmental
policies appeared limited or ill-defined. On such policies, the director
of R&D and corporate affairs stated:

Well, we have an environment policy. We have our obligations under NPC. We have an ingredient selection policy which I sort of see as part of the environment. We have policies on animal testing and the use of animal products.

Supplier policy

When asked what sort of control or requirements Herbal Life imposed on suppliers for environmental issues, the director R&D and corporate affairs replied: 'not a lot.' The COO and general manager observed that Herbal Life's policies and processes were not developed in this area and probably had a limited impact on actual supplier selection, stating:

It's certainly an area we have looked at [imposing environmental requirements on suppliers]. We're not terrifically sophisticated in that area ... we have an audit team that actually go out and review all our suppliers. Part of what they're charged to do is actually look at the environmental aspect. The area – I mean, to be honest it's the bleeding obvious at the moment in terms of we're not finding a terrifically sophisticated environment so I suppose what we'd be basically saying is that we are seeing some gross issues that would make it unacceptable for them to be a supplier and the answer is where we see it, we don't use them. We are saying, 'Well, this one has this environmental footprint and they've got these environmental practices, and this one is 5 per cent better' ... I think it's more of a threshold decision than a fine tuning.

And further:

What I'm saying is it doesn't become, 'Well, we've got two Australian suppliers and this one has this much in carbon emission and this one has this, and so we'll use the lower one'. It's not as fine-tuned around that. But if we had one that said, 'Oh, we're environmentally irresponsible and [one that said] we're very environmentally responsible', we'd use the environmentally responsible one all the time. I mean it just doesn't make sense for the brand not to.

On the same matter, the director of R&D and corporate affairs stated:

We have contact with our suppliers and we do measure, but again our suppliers are basically pills in buckets. I'm trying to think outside of our footprint here. But it's bottles and pills and buckets basically ... we control the quality of what goes into the products from an individual raw material point of view, from a stability point of view. When you put all that stuff together, from keeping moisture out of it and all that sort of stuff, we control the source in terms of quality. I mean oils ain't oils, you know, there's good and bad ...

I think we had that era of low cost manufacture and that still drives some of that culture in purchasing to the point where, in our industry, a lot of companies are going to India and China. We now deal with Chinese raw material manufacturers – or we specify their material. Whereas probably, you know eight or ten years ago, we certainly wouldn't have done that. So cost and accounting does come into purchasing ...

Indonesia is a good example because [the company] probably never thought about asking them if they use child labour in producing those sorts of products. I know a couple of people who have been there and subconsciously if it was happening they would have come back and probably said something about it.

Development of sustainability indicators

Respondents stated that very few sustainability indicators had been developed by Herbal Life. The corporate communications manager did note one indicator the company was trying to develop:

> Basically since we present to the board each year, what we're planning to do with our sponsorship budget and one of the things that we were challenged by [the chairman of the board] to do, which we have now done and we're waiting on at the moment – we haven't actually reported this back to the board yet – was how do we rate compared to other companies, as far as what proportion of our profit we donate back to the community? And we've actually now been able to consolidate and capture [that information] because it's not like we just go to a little pool of money and that's it. I mean, we capture some things, like Arthritis Australia might be supported out of a budget that includes the promotion of products that are for arthritis. And they wouldn't be captured in the same one as my pool of money that I look after, which is sometimes a little more philanthropic.

In terms of whether GRI indicators were being considered as a possible framework for sustainability reporting, the corporate communications manager said, 'No, to be honest, we haven't even had a conversation about it'.

With regard to what the company does report, the corporate communications manager stated:

Look, I think if there were two things: one, we have a responsibility to get back to shareholders and tell them how we're spending their money and that's part of it. And the other thing is we're trying to paint a picture, because it's not just shareholders that read the annual report. It's everyone from people that might be going for a job here, to companies that we might be considering partnering with, to students doing assignments, to journalists that might be writing a story on Herbal Life. I mean, it is quite a wide audience that would have access to this the annual report. So we're also trying to paint a picture, and not an unrealistic one, of what sort of attitude we have on some of these [sustainability] issues ... the last thing we also want to do is window dress some of the initiatives to the point where we're creating an unrealistic picture of what actually happens because a significant number of our shareholders are staff. And the last thing we want, and we're very conscious of this on the staff relations issue, that they read about 'we've got a gym and we do this and we've got a separate area for that and we give you profit and all of that'. And someone reads it and goes, 'it's just not like that'. So we do want ... it to be an accurate portrayal of what it is. So there's two-fold to it. One is it is straight out reporting, we have a responsibility to report on what we've been doing with shareholders' money. And, on the other side, to really try and promote the business, leverage some of the opportunities that we've had, promote the brand position positively. All those things.

SECTION THREE

Stakeholder engagement

For Herbal Life, many respondents could not identify a clear stakeholder group for the company's sustainability initiatives. When asked who the company's major stakeholders for sustainability information were, the director of operations stated:

> I'm just trying to think who they'd be. I'm struggling with that one. We've got a website that's visited by people who might even not take Herbal Life products, who look into it.

The director of operations seemed to suggest that the actual practice of sustainability within the organisation was more important than public image:

> I guess what I'm saying is that there are people who actually are the real McCoy, there are people that want you to think that they're the real McCoy and there are people that just aren't the real McCoy who just say that they are. I'd like to think that Herbal Life are somewhere down here in the real McCoy.

While many respondents could not identify clear stakeholder groups, there was a general consensus that the company's sustainability initiatives were very good for the image of the business. The corporate communications manager stated:

> Where it becomes relevant to sustainability is there are people that love Herbal Life, they really adore us as a company. And they love hearing that we're doing good things. And they love all of that. And we know that because we can track how long they spend in the newsletter and how many of them

open the stories about Herbal Life compared to the general population that, to be honest, they're really not interested in. And we know that because we can tell that they don't open the stories, they don't spend long reading them and we can evaluate all those different things. So the Herbal Life stories on sustainability and the pat on the back stories and all those sorts of things we do tend to target towards the audiences we know find that information relevant.

He also said:

We've actually got a very small shareholder base and it's very thinly traded our stock. And so for that reason, appealing to a lot of the investor groups and the analysts and all those sorts of things probably aren't as important a priority to us. We've got a great share price at the moment and all of those sorts of things [so we're] just getting on with business and doing the best job we can.

The Corporate Communications Manager stated:

I think it's a chance for us to step it up a notch. And I think also, winning the sustainability award, we actually got a lot of great publicity. It generated a lot of really good feeling amongst staff and we were really proud to win it. And it was a really good talking point with our retailers and all of that sort of stuff. Our share price definitely did well around that time. And I think it was a really good reminder there actually is a real benefit to us nurturing this area of the business. So I think there'd be a real commitment to us stepping it up to the next level.

SECTION FOUR

Hurdles facing the collection, integration and reporting of sustainability information

Respondents identified several hurdles facing the effective collection, integration and reporting of sustainability information. One fundamental issue that surfaced with some respondents was defining the whole concept of sustainability and what it means to an organisation in a practical sense. For instance, the chairman of the board stated:

> The moment you mention sustainability, I think of environmental issues, environmental sustainability. I don't think initially about the sustainability of the business as such, which I know you're also considering. The moment I hear the word sustainability, my focus now starts on the new – we're building a new site. Are we worried about the water reticulation and all that? That's my first impression of sustainability. I think the expression is obviously much broader and wider and whether you're building sustainable business practices and all those sort of things. So we'll allude to that but you just might find it hard to get me down that path.

Another major hurdle brought up by several respondents is resource and time constraints to collect and report on sustainability information. In particular, companies tend to be pre-occupied with other priorities, such as the traditional reporting function. The chairman of the board stated:

> Well I think the problem you've got with this is that most companies are snowed by reporting issues and now you're

going to say, 'I want you to do this as well. We've come up with a new way to measure sustainability in your organisation and we're going to have a sustainability report.' 'Oh God', is most people's reaction. 'Oh, not something else, it's just too hard. Go away and leave us alone. Let us get on with our bloody life for crying out loud. Don't put more imposition on us.' So that's a hurdle that you're going to have to think about.

The corporate communications manager stated:

When you consider the amount of resources that it would take to do that [report on sustainability information], and we do have a finite amount of resources for all that we do, we need to consider – and that's where I think the directive comes not from me probably but more the executive committee – whether or not this is the direction that we go. Because we just need to be careful that we're not spending more time putting in place the bureaucracy, if that's all it's going to be doing and, ... so, if in putting together a sustainability report we've still only got the same number of people that we do and, putting in place all the measures, say for example as paper, I mean it sounds like a really simple thing but to actually implement that as a business takes people's time, all those sorts of things. I would hate to think that any of that would take away from some of the things that we are doing ...

I think reporting and knowing that people are accountable motivates people into action. And that, in itself, is a good thing. As long as we're not spending too much time getting caught up in the bureaucracy of it. So, the correct answer, in my opinion, is somewhere between the two worlds. It's not on our agenda as much as it probably should be.

Measurement considerations were considered a major hurdle, particularly in terms of putting a value on people. The chairman of the board stated:

> My IT manager is sitting down with me the other day and I said, 'When you go back to that IT department after this meeting ... I want you to just look at the people around the room and imagine that they've got a number on their forehead, two million bucks, because that's what they cost this company. So how the hell can you justify when you want to buy a new forklift that you give me ten pages of argument but you don't do that with the people.' So that's a system of trying, in my view, to put a realistic number. Now just start adding up how many people you've got in the organisation and multiply that by a million or two million bucks and then compare that with how much bricks and mortar and stuff you've got in the place and then you've got a real system of accounting. That's what you guys need to do, because what it's all about is putting a dollar value on things. That's what accounting is all about, putting a dollar value on things.

A case study analysis of Local Leader

Background of Local Leader

Local Leader, as a local government council, oversees one of Australia's largest city centres and several inner suburbs. Compared to many other local councils in Australia, particularly urban councils servicing large populations, Local Leader is in a strong financial position. In recent years it has maintained a strong net working capital position, significant cash assets, large accumulated surpluses and zero interest-bearing debt. While Local Leader provides an extensive range of services to its municipality, rates revenue has been maintained at modest CPI levels, and projected rates increases are under Local Leader's employee costs of five per cent and only slightly higher than its projected investment return of four per cent.

Regulatory environment of Local Leader

As a local government authority, Local Leader operates under state-specific legislation for local councils, such as the state-based Local Government Act. The legislation provides a framework by which councils must provide services to their respective communities. The legislation introduced six principles to which every council must adhere in delivering services to its community. Councils must also provide a range of planning and accountability reports. The Act requires that all local governments, including Local Leader, must prepare and approve a council plan. A council plan must include, among other things:

- the strategic objectives of the council
- strategies for achieving the objectives for at least the next four years

- strategic indicators for monitoring the achievement of the objectives
- a strategic resource plan.

Why Local Leader was selected for a case study

Local Leader was selected as a case study due to its established corporate reputation as a leader in the sustainability field. Local Leader has a wide and varied range of sustainability policies and initiatives. Environmental policies include ambitious targets to reduce greenhouse gas emissions, water usage, and waste generation. Local Leader's Environment Management Plan sets out a number of waste and environmental practices for all properties in the municipality and applies to all property owners and occupiers. Its objective is to promote a 'safe, cleaner and more pleasant environment in their city and surrounds'. Local Leader's Greenhouse Action Plan sets out strategies to reduce greenhouse gas emissions across the municipality to zero by 2020 and is maintaining a high public profile in terms of leadership towards future sustainability, particularly with respect to climate change. Among Local Leader's environmental strategies is a water catchment strategy, which seeks local solutions to water management issues. In this space, Local Leader is developing ways of using storm water run-off from roads and footpaths, capturing rain from rooftops and improving the water quality in waterways.

Local Leader also has a sustainable waste management strategy focused on recycling. As stated in its annual report, the 'major purpose is to empower people working, visiting and living in the city to "do more with less" – by avoiding the creation of waste in the first place.'

Other sustainability policies include parks policies and plans and sustainable public lighting. Local Leader also has a number of internal policies and initiatives, such as; the implementation of a sustainability purchasing policy; policies on the use of recycled paper; the use of hybrid cars for its vehicle fleet; developing the 'City Index'; and the construction of an energy-efficient building with an emphasis on the wellbeing of occupants.

The organisational structure of Local Leader also highlights the council's emphasis on sustainability. The CEO is responsible for establishing and maintaining an organisational structure that ensures the decisions of Local Leader are implemented, and that the day-to-day management of the council's operations are in accordance with the council plan. The CEO also provides timely advice to the council. The office of the CEO liaises with the offices of the Lord Mayor and Deputy Lord Mayor, councillors, Local Leader executives, state government and key community and corporate stakeholders to ensure council's strategic objectives are met using all available resources. The Office of the Lord Mayor provides high level advisory and administrative support services for the operation of the offices of the Lord Mayor and Deputy Lord Mayor. The Chief of Staff, along with support staff, works closely with the offices of the CEO, councillor support, directors and managers to ensure an effective relationship exists to support the functionality of the council.

Sustainability has an important role in the overall organisational structure of Local Leader. For instance, the Division of Sustainability and Regulatory Services sits directly under the CEO. Within the structure of Local Leader there is a series of special and advisory committees, including the Eco-City Committee which was established to facilitate one of Local Leader's key visions on sustainability. The Eco-City Committee (published on the organisation's website) has been delegated the powers, duties and functions directly relating or ancillary to:

> air quality, enhancing environmental partnerships, greenhouse emissions, climate change, Sustainable City Fund, waste management and minimisation, public

space (including parklands and trees), parks and waters (environment), water conservation and quality including stormwater management and the Local Environmental initiatives.

Local Leader also has a 'continuous improvement' program based on 'Lean Thinking', which aims to eliminate waste in its processes to provide value to customers. The sustainability initiatives of the continuous improvement team include 'Local Leader Green', a staff-driven program to improve workplace sustainability. The program harnesses staff enthusiasm for reducing Local Leader's environmental footprint as an organisation and a municipality. As an organisation-wide plan for an environmentally sustainable workplace, Local Leader Green aligns with the Future Community Plan vision of an Eco-City: a city where people and organisations adapt to a changing climate and gladly act to build a sustainable future. Planned projects under Local Leader Green include the Clinton Climate Initiative Building Retrofit Program, improving energy and water efficiency and the sustainability behaviours of staff at 15 of the organisation's most energy- and water-intensive buildings; and sharing lessons and knowledge, continuing to maximise the impact of Local Leader Green activities by working alongside other organisations.

Local Leader's current council plan places a strong emphasis on establishing key sustainable objectives and performance targets to meet these objectives. For instance, under the Eco-City goal, key objectives include:

- influencing the municipality to become a zero net emissions city
- influencing the municipality to achieve total water catchment
- influencing the municipality to use resources efficiently
- promoting and advocating for the production, supply and purchase of local food

- influencing the municipality to adapt to climate change
- influencing the municipality to use less portable (drinking) water
- educating the community about environmental issues
- aiming to become a centre for excellence in sustainable design and management
- becoming recognised as a world leader in climate change adaptation through innovative solutions.

In terms of the measurables, Local Leader has set strategic indicators around objectives, such as:

- Local Leader's performance on refuse recycling initiatives and effective and efficient water usage
- CO_2 emissions per resident per year
- CO_2 emissions per worker per year
- tonnes of greenhouse gas emissions for the municipality per year
- the percentage of municipal waste diverted for recycling
- the reduction of residential waste to landfill per household
- the reduction of greenhouse gas emissions from council operations
- the reduction of waste to landfill from council facilities (offices)
- the number of commercial buildings retrofitted under the 1200 program
- the reduction of drinking-quality water consumed for council buildings and gardens.

Respondents selected for the case study

Respondents were drawn from a wide cross-section of the organisation and involved 17 interviews averaging approximately one hour each. Interviewees included respondents with the following occupations: director, finance and administration; executive general manager, strategic communications; executive manager, systems; group environmental manager; group financial accountant; group knowledge manager; group manager, occupational health and safety; group plant manager; group safety manager; group strategic sourcing manager; HR manager, corporate; information systems manager; management accountant; manager, greenhouse and energy; OHS manager, systems and compliance; safety systems co-ordinator; and senior environmental adviser, business services.

Outline of case study

The remainder of this case is organised as follows:

Section one explores some of the issues surrounding the public image of sustainability projected by Local Leader and the perceptions of sustainability reporting by respondents working daily with the programs and initiatives within the organisation.

Section two explores Local Leader's processes, systems and methodologies for the collection, integration and reporting of sustainability information.

Section three explores the extent to which stakeholder engagement influences or impacts on sustainability reporting practices within the organisation.

Section four discusses potential hurdles confronting the collection, integration and reporting of sustainability information with the organisation.

Finally, some conclusions and policy implications are considered.

SECTION ONE

Public image versus internal perceptions

While the interview questions brought out a healthy level of scepticism among many respondents, particularly among accountants, many respondents who were interviewed showed a genuine level of engagement and interest in the sustainability issues raised in the interview questions. Notwithstanding some significant differences of opinion across respondents, several respondents showed a high level of support and enthusiasm for the various sustainability programs, activities and initiatives of Local Leader. There was also a strong sense among some respondents that the organisation is 'getting somewhere' on its sustainability agenda, albeit in a slow and rather chaotic manner. The sense of tangible achievement was more palpable in some respondents than others. For instance, the procurement coordinator marvelled at Local Leader's recent initiative on recycled paper:

> Let me talk about our recycled paper. We've done really well. We used to buy Evolve, remember the old Evolve paper. Evolve comes from the UK of course and we have been using that for the last five years and we were looking for an alternative. Australia didn't have a 100 per cent recycled paper so when we heard the Australian Paper Mills had come up with the Reflex 100 – you're familiar with that – we went down to Marysville … We went down for the day and it was a long drive. We went down there and had a look at the plant. We were really impressed with the whole plant and the way they went about it and it was equivalent – we weighed it up with what was happening with Evolve. So our line is instead of getting paper from 17,000 kilometres away, we get it from

[less than 1000] kilometres away ... it's good for landfill in Australia. So we're not sort of helping the Europeans out; we're helping Australian landfill. So it's a win-win for the organisation and it was also about 50 cents cheaper a ream and that was all good, good, good. You know all the ticks in boxes and we did really well with that.

There is no doubt that initiatives such as Local Leader's green energy-efficient building have had some impact on sustainability culture at Local Leader. For some respondents, this was the physical manifestation of sustainability for the world to see. As stated by the director of sustainability:

Building the new building is a physical demonstration of all these things coming into play. Three councils' back [they] made a decision that they would not only build a new office building for staff, but they would deliberately try and create something that would be a demonstration project for the rest of the community and were prepared to spend a little bit more on that. Now, that's quite a long way back in this journey and it was at a time when things like the triple bottom line were still swirling around, but they made that decision and it's paid off in spades, frankly. I mean, the impact that that building has had, internally and externally, is profound and a lot of our staff are now living the experience of this notion of transformation to a new future. So, as we go along, it's becoming more and more part of the fabric, but not just through organisational means. It's the doing of it that works for an organisation like ours.

Notwithstanding Local Leader's real commitment to sustainability as a concept, one of the intriguing themes to emerge from the Local Leader case analysis is a conspicuous discrepancy between the perception or public persona of sustainability projected by Local Leader in its corporate image and the reality of sustainability as a rigorous measurement and reporting process within the organisation itself. As respondents pointed out, Local Leader shows plenty of visible manifestations of sustainability. As stated by the manager of continuous improvement:

> You've got this building, we've got our fleet vehicles, and we went for early adoption ... of the Prius hybrid electric technology in cars just to get it out there so we could display it and invite examination, invite discussion.

However, while Local Leader has carefully cultivated its image as a leading protagonist of sustainability culture and practice, many respondents believe the collection, measurement and reporting of the sustainability data does not live up to the organisation's lofty public image. Practice lags the image, in some cases, by significant margins. As stated by the group accountant, the construction of a green-star building distracts attention from the underlying measurement flaws in the organisation:

> We fought very hard not to sign up [to sustainability data collection]. As finance we fought – because it was a requirement for us to do a lot of this reporting that we just didn't have the mechanisms to capture that information. So it's a very, very, very manual process. We got away with it the last couple of years because we've got this beautiful [green-star] building and so we can just put all that in and that sort of blows everyone away. But underneath we don't have the measuring.

Notwithstanding Local Leader's strong public image in sustainability, the continuous improvement consultant acknowledged that staff awareness of sustainability was generally low throughout the organisation, a situation seemingly at odds with Local Leader's official image, stating:

> We've been on the sustainability journey for some time now. However, there has been recognition from our last staff culture survey that staff awareness of sustainability probably isn't as high as what it should be. So, we're probably at a point where we need to rejuvenate that, which is what the [sustainability] blueprint is currently looking at now.

As might be expected, there was some divergence of opinion among respondents. On the surface, accountants tended to take a more cynical view of sustainability, but on closer analysis this cynicism could relate in part to the frustrations of getting the hard data they need for measurement and reporting; and the lack of focus within the organisation on defining sustainability within manageable and measureable parameters or boundaries. The group accountant noted that there had been a lot of selling of the corporate sustainability image, but the measurement credentials were simply not there. He stated: 'I think it's good PR. Someone's done a good sell job out there, absolutely a good sell job, [but] the processes we have don't support it.'

And further:

> So it's a little bit frightening when one of the directors goes off and talks about sustainability ... you'd better be careful what you say because people will think, 'we'll come there and find out that you've done all these wonderful things' and we have, in fairness, we've probably done some good things. Certainly as far as the energy side of things ... and measuring that and tracking down and making sure our water consumption

reduces and things like that. I think they've done some really good work.

Respondents with accounting backgrounds tended to be more sensitive to the inherent lack of verifiability and timeliness of sustainability data and the perception that information relating to sustainability is too 'soft' to report on. Interestingly, this view was also held by some respondents who did not hold an accounting role within Local Leader. The divisional business coordinator (sustainable development and strategy) implied that Local Leader's commitment to a sustainability report was haphazard and more for show as there was no serious concern expressed by the preparers about the relevance and reliability of the underlying data:

> Now, the one [sustainability report] we actually published last year was the first one that got published but it was actually the second report. The first report got binned because it got sent to the external auditors who said, 'You can't justify the data.' We said, 'What do you mean we can't, the data is data.' [They responded] 'Yes, but how did you get there? We want to see the audit trails to get to that point.' So instead of giving them the audit trails, what we did is we said, 'Okay, well let us take that data and here is a new set of data. But this isn't the same as that. We'll put that in the report, we will support this lot.' They said, 'Well okay, take that one away' because they could not support the data with it. So, [we said], 'What we will do this time, we have learned a lot and we will put in a report.' It never saw the light of day. Then it sort of died ... and then about the middle of April – no it was early May last year – [name suppressed] made a pronouncement that, yes, we were going to have a sustainability report for that year. So he formed a group of people from right across the corporation

to come together to compile and publish the sustainability report and I went along for the first working group meeting and there were representatives from all across the divisions. There were people there from the centre for TRI [toxics release inventory] reporting at ICLEI [International Council for Local Environmental Initiatives] and they all had this great agenda that in six weeks' time we were going to be in a position to send off this report and I'm going, 'Hang on a minute, for what year?' They said, 'Well, this year', and I said, 'And how are you going to get the data, how are you going to have all the audit trail?' [They said,] 'Won't be a problem'. I said, 'Right now, as it stands six weeks out, you haven't even got the strands identified, never mind the data to support, answer the questions and support it'. 'Oh, won't be a problem', they said. [To which I replied], 'Yes, it will be a problem', because I had been going through the new GRI format and I said, 'Well, we didn't make the last one by a country mile, how do you think you are going to make this new one?' 'It's all under control.'

So they started working through it and the problem became evident very quickly that while we had a huge amount of data, it didn't fit. 'So, okay', [they said], 'What can we report on, what can we make fit?' I said, 'But that's not the point'. I got put in a cubby hole as almost the troublemaker because I was looking at things ... I put it to the guy from ECOSYS, I said to him the problem was we have got a whole lot of output measures and a whole lot of output data and we are measuring this way and we have got to produce a sustainability report that is supposed to talk about outcomes ... [the response] was basically, 'What's wrong with that?' I said, 'If you are going to report on outcomes, you have outcome measures and you have outcome data against those measures ... you have got data and you have got measures but I don't think they are actually measuring the right things'.

Local Leader's previous experience with TBL reporting also weighed on many responses. Some respondents perceived TBL to be an 'off the shelf model' which was not (or could not be) integrated well within the strategic directions and operations of Local Leader. As stated by the manager of continuous improvement:

It's the approach that I feel is best and in some respects there might be a sense that we've moved backwards from the TBL because you know we were kind of out there with TBL toolkits and, you know, advertising ourselves very strongly. But I felt that it was ... artificial is a really good word, that's exactly how I felt it was. There was just this artificial layer that was not actually in any way related to what we were doing and, you know, for me I always think that that's just a waste.

The divisional business coordinator (sustainable development and strategy) also considered TBL to be a quick fix solution to sustainability, stating:

I think the thing was that when we went with TBL, they went with TBL because the then TBL coordinator saw it as an off the shelf model that you can, yep, buy that, put it in the computer and run it.

The experience with TBL was viewed quite negatively by some accounting respondents. The manager of financial services stated:

And that's the experience that we've had because we have had attempts at introducing a TBL approach to our capital works program, for example, but I think it lost a bit of credibility ...

> mainly because the numbers are not considered objective ...
> when it gets to that, you know how you measure the social
> impact and environmental impact, often it's not as ... there's
> no hard measure.

As a result of the negativity, Local Leader gradually moved
away from a rigid application of the TBL approach to measuring
sustainability against its six strategic objectives laid out in the council
plan. Respondents indicated that the main focus has been to make
the TBL approach or philosophy work contextually for Local Leader.
The manager of continuous improvement stated:

> Our challenge, for us, we've really always tried to make
> it relevant to the organisation I would say into what we're
> doing. So even with the framework, we used to have a TBL
> kind of approach. We've kind of tended to drop that a little
> bit and talk about our own strategic objectives which have a
> TBL sort of philosophy underpinning them anyway.

The immense challenges of sustainability and the seeming
mismatch between Local Leader's public image and the reality of
sustainability within the organisation was aptly described by the
director of sustainability:

> When we're talking about a city, you're talking about the most
> complex thing that human beings have ever created. So, for
> me, it's always been the journey towards sustainability. Some
> people say you should be able to define the final end, the
> destination. I don't think you can when you're dealing with
> something as complex as a city, but ... you know when you're
> moving in that direction if you've got sufficient antennae
> around as to what the key issues are and, fundamentally, any
> city that's been created in the industrial age has got to be, to

some degree, unsustainable because it's built upon a set of resource inputs that are finite. So … this is the sort of thing that motivates me.

SECTION TWO

Sustainability: data collection, measurement and reporting

It was clear from interviews with a range of respondents that Local Leader possessed a wide array of sophisticated information systems (including accounting systems). From an accounting systems perspective, Local Leader evidently had the capacity to collect a broad and complex array of financial and non-financial data. For instance, according to respondents, Local Leader used sophisticated packages such as Oracle for financials and GA Pathway for rates processing, parking infringements, building and planning permits and approvals. Orion was used for HR and document management under Hummingbird, and Infomaster was being introduced as a new asset managing system. Stark Essentials was the principal software used by Local Leader to capture carbon emissions.

At least two interesting themes emerged from the interviews with respondents. The first is that while Local Leader appeared to have a vast array of systems to collect a vast amount of data, it was apparent there was very little integration in the systems used.

Respondents suggested there were at least 112 databases for asset information alone across the organisation. As stated by the divisional business coordinator (sustainability and regulatory services):

> That's the major ones but there are also all these transactional databases that are kind of bolted onto it. They'll take a copy of the data and run over to this database and start generating transactions. So it was just a massive amount and that's not where all the qualitative information was being stored, about what decisions were being made from a business plan point of view, what information we gathered about customer service and surveys etc.

The divisional business coordinator (sustainability and regulatory services) described the problems of trying to track carbon emissions to individual asset classes and integrate information across databases:

> One of them is relating to CO_2, energy and water consumption. There is software that we are utilising, Stark Essentials … that just sits off the asset. And one of the things we wanted to really drive was that any data that we collect about energy consumption or generation – water consumption or generation because we're doing both of those now – needs to be assigned to that asset so that we know how that asset performs. Once again, it's this thing of creating that loop in procurement. How well is that type of building performing compared to this building? And this goes back to the very interesting thing about the replacement for the financial system not incorporating non-financial things. One of the things that was on the table very early on was that it would incorporate particularly energy and water consumption; and for one reason or another, that's fallen off the agenda on that system.

A second theme to emerge among respondents was a lack of understanding or even awareness of key databases utilised by Local Leader. This point was highlighted by the divisional business coordinator (sustainability and regulatory services) in relation to the Stark software, who stated:

> Well, here is an indication of the situation. There is a group called Asset Services that were responsible for developing Stark, which was going to be a sustainability reporting data collection tool. [The director of sustainability] didn't even know about the existence of Stark until a couple of weeks ago. Best kept secret in the world because this particular

area ... they were working on sustainable asset management and I am looking at it and thinking 'whoop di'. Now these little people have got their ovens sitting over in the corner, everything has been thrown in the pot and they are doing all the cooking and not talking to anybody about it. Even the director of sustainability does not even know the thing exists and we were actually going into a model – we were designing a spec for a new financial management reporting system and they got together some financial divisional coordinators and they were saying they wanted to capture this, this, this and this. They said that was about all we need. I was sitting there thinking, 'What about sustainability reporting?'. [To which the response was:] 'What?' I said, 'Well wouldn't it be a logical point to actually capture off the accounts water consumption, power consumption, gas emissions?'

Lack of understanding or skill in using or interrogating databases was also highlighted in the responses. For instance, the team leader for OHS and wellbeing stated:

There has not been any attempt in the past. Just this morning, as part of this GRI, we're looking at how we're pulling data out of Orion. We didn't have the skillset to actually get information out of Orion so that's why we've been running those manual systems. We've now got a report that's actually dropping out the cost of that so we do now have a mechanism of, or a means of, this is what it has cost us this month in WorkCover. We haven't had that before and our area hasn't been reporting against it specifically.

The team leader for OHS and wellbeing also identified gaps in the information systems being used:

> We've got the plaques on the wall but, if you start digging
> down through the layers, there are more gaps that appear in
> that process so it's actually closing those gaps to get a robust
> system. So when you've got that you get your lead indicators
> and you're not looking at the lag. We've got a couple in there
> but not as many as we'd like but it's competing for the front
> page. It's difficult to ... get people on the same page when
> there are lots of sustainability projects.

It is not surprising from the interviews that numerous respondents indicated that sustainability data collection and measurement within the organisation is sometimes haphazard, uncoordinated and ineffective.

Measurement has not been the foundation of Local Leader's reporting culture. The senior consultant for corporate planning and reporting said:

> We've actually, for several years, had quite a strong culture
> of monitoring reporting and accountability. I think that
> culture is quite strong. But measurement using measures
> and targets hasn't been as strong. Monitoring of outputs and
> projects and strategies has been strong and activities. Actual
> measurement hasn't been strong.

There are many tangible examples. For instance, despite Local Leader's public claims of reducing greenhouse emissions (and published performance targets), respondents believed that Local Leader had quite inadequate procedures of measuring CO_2 emissions. The manager, financial services stated:

> There is no obvious way that I can say, well we're managing
> sustainability across the organisation in terms of greenhouse
> gas [emissions]. We are measuring some things, but I don't

know that that's actually brought itself back into actual
management.

In terms of energy and water usage, the divisional business
coordinator (sustainability and regulatory services) stated:

> [We are] pretty much doing a manual interrogation of Oracle
> financials to get energy and water purchases and those
> invoices are being scanned and retained within our document
> management system as verifiable records. The consumption
> data is being extracted and entered into an Excel spread
> sheet. That's being uploaded into Stark Essentials, which will
> retain for every invoice amount those details, the document
> reference, where that invoice could be ...

In terms of energy usage, a major part of the problem is that
utility companies do not provide the necessary information. The
group accountant stated:

> I've tried to talk to utility companies to see if we can get this
> stuff electronically so people don't actually have to key it,
> we could just upload – really, really tough to get [the energy
> usage data]. They've just not got the systems. We went to one
> organisation and they said, 'well give us $10 000 and we'll
> think about it'.

Many respondents indicated that information systems are
not well integrated and do not capture non-financial information
effectively. The group accountant stated:

> Accounts payable, accounts receivable, purchasing, general
> ledger are all Oracle integrated ... now in saying that, we've
> got rates which are a huge revenue for us, and also parking
> fines. They're a different system, so they're not integrated

to our system. We've got a lot of other little bits and pieces around the countryside that aren't integrated.

The divisional business coordinator (sustainable development and strategy) stated:

> Basically that's what we're doing, just emissions at the moment and the way we're gathering it, it's convoluted because we key all our invoices into Oracle and Oracle payments, but to get the information out of Oracle, we don't get a download or anything from Oracle because it can't talk to Stark in any shape or form. So what we have to do is get hard copies of the invoices, scan them, then re-key them … Fred Flintstone could design a better system but this is what we've got, we've got to do it this way until we can come up with a better way. I dropped a bombshell when I said, 'Okay, that's fine for us as a corporation, we're relatively small. Come 1 July next year, we could have to report on our subsidiaries and our legal opinion says that we do have to and they're even less ready than we are'. They're going, 'Well, when are we actually going to get the resources to do this properly?'

For instance, information relating to human resources, financial and sustainability all come from different sources. The procurement coordinator highlighted the lack of integration in systems, saying:

> That's where we want to be. At the moment it's so inconsistent and so [the manager of financial services] can't be comfortable that people will manage things completely because they're managing things in a different way … and mistakes get made. As soon as somebody dumps it into a spread sheet somebody invariably does something. We would love to eliminate all spread sheets. It won't happen, but that would

be the objective. Get rid of all the administrative processes, that's my objective. We will work there over time. Certainly as part of this process we will be refining ... [and] redefining a number of roles.

Further, the divisional business coordinator (sustainability and regulatory services) stated:

Well I think there are four major systems that form up part of the whole equation here, which is currently we've got the Oracle financial, we've got Stark Essentials, which is the repository for our utilities data so the energy usage etc., Asset Master, which I guess is the operational component of the assets and Interplan I see also as the tool whereby we're managing the day-to-day strategic planning of how we're going to implement things. It would be fair to say that all four of those have been generated individually, aware of each other but certainly not built on a firm foundation of interaction. And I think that's still stumping us a little bit on how we can get them really a lot more integrated.

The counterintuitive theme that emerged among respondents was that Local Leader was more focused on services than costs. The group accountant stated:

Child care is probably a really good example because they did that analysis because they want to build a lot more childcare centres. They actually did find all our childcare centres were making huge losses and council has said, 'That's okay because it's a community service and we're prepared to put the money in there to support those'. That sort of level of costing wouldn't drive decisions.

In this sense, internal accounting systems such as ABC or ABM are really used by the Local Leader at a macro level or, in the words of the group accountant, 'a way for analysis and it's a way of reporting to the community, because what happens with these activities, is they summarise the key service outputs that then summarise to a service'.

There was some cynicism within Local Leader about the value and practicality of non-financial information. The group accountant said:

> Ten years ago or more they used to do a very detailed non-financial report to council but it was 50 or 60 pages long and it used to take almost the whole month to compile. By the time they presented it, it was out of date and it was just way too long for people to read. So they got rid of it. This is, if you like, the budget that they did. I imagine that they do a monthly report against this. Every single service is detailed and they had measures for every service. So it was really detailed and really very good. What you really need from this is what are the key half dozen things that really drive your business and put that up to Council. Getting people to agree on that ... we gave up in the end, it was just impossible. Because people are really passionate about what they're doing and if they couldn't see their little bit they thought, I don't think it's good.

However, there also didn't appear to be a strong cultural interest in financial information. The group accountant stated:

> I don't think our reporting is very good at all. The organisation and the councillors are not interested in financial information at all ... if you could tie your financials up into your non-financial information and show that by having 1000

employees that are actually driving your financial cost, then they might be a little bit more interested.

One reason for this apparent lack of interest is that Local Leader is financially strong. In the context of whether state government would be interested in financial performance measures, the group accountant stated:

> I guess they'd be very interested if we didn't have a lot of money in the bank. We've got a lot of money in the bank so they're not very interested. All they're interested in is how much money we're going to give them, which we continue to do, we continue to give them money. That's another issue, whereby we're not going to have much money left in the bank if we continue to give state government a lot of our money.

The divisional business coordinator (sustainable development and strategy) stated that, to some extent, data collection and measurement was hindered by outside sources. In terms of collecting water usage and energy usage, the respondent stated:

> We collect it. We get the retailer to give it to us. We actually go to them [the retailers] separately. For example, the sustainability report, we actually went back to them and said, 'Can you review your records and tell us how much water we have used?'. The timing was horrendous. The first time we did the sustainability report even the auditor – because we actually have got it in some of the corporate reports – said they were going to tag the thing saying we had used 12-month-old data in a corporate external report.

However, some of the obstacles in data collection and measurement were internal. Attempts to get sustainability information from the accountants had not previously been successful. The divisional business coordinator (sustainable development and strategy) stated:

> We formalised the request and put it up to the manager, financial services. It came back with a red line through it: 'I'm not prepared to slow down my accounts payable process to record data for you guys to complete your sustainability report or your emissions report or whatever it might be'.

Another aspect of lack of integration is that Local Leader does not report on its subsidiaries. For instance, a separate subsidiary entity was formed in 1993, owned by Local Leader, to provide services to the city. However, since 1994 the subsidiary started competing for other council works as a subsidiary of Local Leader. Failure to include that subsidiary's footprint was perceived by respondents to undermine the reliability of Local Leader's carbon emission reporting. The divisional business coordinator (sustainable development and strategy) stated:

> Of the nine councillors we've got, at least three are saying our sustainability report is inadequate because it doesn't report on the subsidiaries at all. The comment was made at the time, 'We'll get the corporation reporting right first and then we'll bring the others on'. My basic comment was, 'We need to walk before we can run'. We were having a problem walking and he [councillor] was going, 'No, no, I want them all in it'. It just wasn't possible.
>
> Sustainability tried to have a meeting with them and then their team leader had one meeting with Citywide and they threw their arms up in horror and said, 'Give us about two years and we'll be on track'. The sustainability team leader said, 'Well, you haven't got two years'. Then he consequently

left. We've only just got a team leader back in the area. Recently, the sustainability team all went off to an emissions trading seminar run by the prime minister's office. It was a sort of road show all around and they all came back and said, 'Oh well, you know we can become a central reporting agency ... we'll use our systems to report not only on our sustainability and our subsidiaries but we'll report on behalf of other councils, because we've got the systems in place'.

Not surprisingly, respondents did not believe sustainability information was embedded in the organisation's decision-making. There was a general feeling that the organisations' sustainability culture would not change while sustainability was not used on a day-to-day decision-making basis, as one responded stated: 'Just doing a yearly report is not getting engagement.' Respondents recognised a need for timely and reliable sustainability information to be communicated to the operational managers. The manager, financial services stated the following with regards to decision-making:

No, I don't think it has got to a point where it's a decision point yet. It's just recording and reporting so that we at least start to accumulate some sort of history. I think that's important too, because part of the problem that you face in trying to work out how you're going forward or how you performed going back is that often there are no records, there is no reliable information available. So consequently you don't know whether to go forward or go back. So irrespective of whether you're using the data – I think if the data is at least reliable and gives some sort of concept or context around what you see as important parts of that sustainability measurement, then I think it's important to collect it.

A good example of how sustainability information was failing to impact decision-making was in Local Leader's sustainable purchasing policy. The manager of financial services stated:

> It would be much better if you had a properly agreed structure and framework in place and if you worked on making sure that the data was available and reliable ... that's what I think creates problems. It's the reliability and the availability of the data. And if you have those two, then you can start making sensible decisions or at least sensible strategies ... I don't know that we actually do have it.

In responding to the question 'How does the organisation judge success or otherwise?' the manager of financial services stated:

> Well I think it's just an implied assumption that the more we buy of green-related products, the better things will be. So I don't know that we're actually doing any more than that really. I mean I could be wrong ... there are bits that we do. It's a good example, the sustainable eco-friendly paper. We look at it and we look at it on the basis of that cost and we've recently just changed one of the principal suppliers. I can't think who it was now, but it's an Australian-based company who now provides the same type of paper on the same basis that we were purchasing previously from overseas. So that's created an interest to look at whether we source this stuff from a cheaper provider. But again, it's not a huge strategy of it's in our backyard, so we do it.

What is interesting is Local Leader appears to have sufficiently robust and sophisticated information systems to collect sustainability data. However, some respondents believed there was no real organisational will to collect the data (possibly because it was not used for decision-making). For instance, the chief information officer stated:

> I mean even today a number of the systems are capable of doing that [collecting sustainability data] but we just haven't asked them to do that. We have the ability to build data marts, collate that information from different sources and pull that together in terms of the one report.
>
> I think what we have got is different work areas have asked for different bits of information, whether it is the electricity or the water, and we are doing those bits but I don't believe we have a general theme which I think is prompting that to be done.

Sustainability reporting

An interesting feature of Local Leader's sustainability reporting at the time of the interviews was the separation of the sustainability report from the annual report. This separation seems counterintuitive to Local Leader's strong cultural and institutional emphasis on sustainability. The reason for separation of the two reports was explained by the continuous improvement consultant:

> What happened this year was we actually separated the sustainability element from this year's annual report. We separated the two and we said we were going to develop a stand-alone sustainability report for this year – one that allows us time to do some thinking around what our goals and aims are. It also allows us the time to invite other staff to be part of the process ... corporate communications were starting their annual report so they couldn't be active in both

camps at the same time. So the continuous improvement branch this year has taken more of a lead role with the sustainability report, which is me. I've been full-time on it for the last two-and-a-half months.

The manager of continuous improvement stated:

The reason we separated it – last year was the first year we had – was driven by the fact that we had made a commitment to GRI more than we had really worked out that this really supported the way we wanted to report. So it was quite difficult for us to try and incorporate the GRI indicators and that's all we were really using last year. You know, the GRI indicators trying to incorporate that into the annual report, created a 168-page, 1.3 kg monster.

At the end of it I felt that we really hadn't understood anything about the GRI. We'd just been pressured into getting the data and making sure that we incorporated it into the report. So we felt that we wanted to get some value out of heading down that line. Myself and the director of corporate performance sat down and we said, 'Look, if we want to head down this way, we really do need to sit down and think about what it is and what value it adds and get a handle on that'. It was too difficult to try to do that while we were sort of desperately trying to get the annual report done because of the whole timeframes associated with the annual report. So we actually felt we would separate it without making a decision about whether we would look to bring it back again together or maintain it separately.

This respondent also explained reasons for duplication in sustainability with annual report:

Now we're at a stage where we're saying we could see a lot of duplication between the annual report and the sustainability report. I think it was because ... when you're reporting you're always reporting against something and the issue [with sustainability] was we didn't have a plan to report against. So what we were using was the council plan and saying, 'Well, right. We'll report against that'. The annual report reports against the council plan. So hence, the duplication was arising from that. So the question really becomes what's the sustainability report reporting against? Maybe that's going to be the CityPlan when the CityPlan is developed, in which case it will report against the city. It will be clearly the city.

SECTION THREE

Stakeholder engagement

Respondents acknowledged that many potential stakeholders were interested in Local Leader's sustainability report. The continuous improvement consultant listed some of these stakeholders: 'They are a whole range of people, not just residents – businesses, investors, government agencies, academic, global, international, national, local; not just local governments – state, Commonwealth, environmental agencies, [and] NGOs.' However, respondents seemed to indicate that there was very little engagement with stakeholders in the development of the sustainability report (notwithstanding that stakeholders have been engaged in other processes of Local Leader, such as budgetary processes).

The manager of continuous improvement stated:

> Yeah, when we were doing this [sustainability] report, we were doing it sort of with G2, but using the draft guidelines for G3. So we've already started down the track and although we didn't do stakeholder consultation developing this report, that was actually a considered decision that we felt we would put the report out first and then we would do the consultation prior to doing our next report.

In developing the sustainability report, respondents indicated that the focus has been internal. The manager of continuous improvement stated:

> The report hasn't been finished yet so while at the beginning of the process we identified certain staff as key stakeholders, and part of the audience from an internal point of view, from an external point of view the decision was made that

we would publish this report, then go out to community consultation earlier next year to test whether or not the issues we have chosen to report on are relevant and material to those stakeholders. That's probably going to shift our thinking for the process next year.

SECTION FOUR

Hurdles facing the collection, integration and reporting of sustainability information

It was clear from several interviews with respondents that Local Leader was facing a number of substantive hurdles in the collection, integration and reporting of sustainability information. Some of these hurdles were organisational, some cultural and political, while others were more of a technical nature (such as data collection constraints). The following section considers some of the hurdles that emerged from the interviews.

Effects of the restructure

Many respondents indicated that the effects of several restructures within Local Leader had a significant negative impact on the internal sustainability efforts of Local Leader, particularly in terms of reduced staff and loss of thought leadership in the area. These concerns were well articulated by the director of sustainability, who said:

> Well, we no longer have a dedicated sustainability branch, so that's the biggest change in this context within the structure. The functions that branch previously undertook have been amalgamated with what were previously the strategic planning group. And also what has been brought into that same group here that won't be evident from [our organisational] chart is the corporate planning function. And one of the recommendations in the consultants' review report – I don't know if you've had the time or the interest or the inclination to have a look at that – was that they recommended that sustainability, as an issue, needed to be more broadly based within the organisation, rather than

being an area of specialisation. Now I don't think it was as black and white as all of that. But, nonetheless, that was the statement made in that report. So going forward, what are the changes? The policy commitments of the council are the same. There's no change to that. The resourcing of those policy commitments is slightly different in that there is no longer a dedicated executive leading that as a single issue. Instead there is a more broadly based branch which has the potential of introducing sustainability concepts into more broadly based strategic planning and corporate planning functions of the council. Now probably the biggest opportunity here is the corporate planning side of it, to integrate word and deed – word in a sense of strategic planning, deed in a sense of corporate planning and its flow on through to the allocation of resources. I should also tell you that this combination actually has existed in the past.

But one of the risks that you have with a small dedicated group is that they're quite vulnerable to a few people suddenly having reason to leave. So in a slightly larger group, hopefully, that's a bit more robust.

According to the divisional business coordinator (sustainable development and strategy):

Sustainability was literally purged of staff, and the ones that didn't get made redundant, left anyway. So at one point it got down to about two staff in the entire branch who were there.

Basically the way the organisation is now structured is that there are the people that do the doing and then the divisional coordinators will be the ones relied upon to try and identify areas for improvement or efficiency or whatever, as well as doing all the other things you're supposed to do. What happened in this particular division, over the course of the restructure when it first started, [the director of sustainability] went from 185 staff down to about 35. He's now gone up to 465. There's now half the council in one division.

Data collection and measurement constraints

As stated by the manager, financial services, 'What's measured is managed. But if we don't measure it, we don't manage it and that's an important thing'. There was a concern among several respondents that measurement constraints could greatly limit the value and practicality of sustainability information. Respondents noted that previous efforts to introduce TBL to capital works programs lost credibility and traction in the organisation because the numbers were perceived as 'soft' (there are no hard measures for social and environmental impacts). The 'tick the box' style exercise and long lists of processes failed and, as stated by the manager of financial services:

> Even if you spend a lot of time on it, because we've done that, we've been down that road and spent an enormous amount of time and really, at the end of the day you just wonder whether any significant change in the actual program has taken place as a consequence of it.

Difficulties in collecting the necessary data were highlighted by several respondents, including the divisional business coordinator (sustainability and regulatory services), who said:

> We have tried on a number of occasions now to get electronic data transferred from the utility companies and it has failed on a number of occasions, which makes this whole process an enormously manual event. Three quarters of invoice

data is input into our finance system; three or four items of consumption and meter readings etc. is not. And a whole other area has to be established to capture that piece of data.

Other respondents identified problems with measuring against the GRI. The manager of continuous improvement stated:

Obviously we have built our sustainability report around the GRI principles and I would also separate out the principles from the indicators. I think I've certainly found the principles exceedingly useful. You know they're probably common sense to a large degree but they really have helped us form our report. The indicators at times are more difficult to work out ... I think that's because you know they're not necessarily built for public sector and we are now starting to use the public sector supplements.

With respect to the sustainable purchasing policy, the group accountant stated:

I've got purchasing under my wing and we have done a sustainability purchasing policy, which essentially sets out to people that you can go out and buy green products, socially responsible products, and you can actually pay a little bit of a premium for doing that because we appreciate that it's going to be a little bit more expensive. So we've got the policy out there but that's as far as we've got so far. We don't have a way of actually measuring how people are progressing against this policy and that's really, I guess, our next step.

Lack of staff awareness on sustainability

Several respondents noted that staff awareness and understanding of sustainability issues was very low in the organisation, which contrasts with the strong sustainability profile of the organisation publicly. This was one of the reasons that some respondents believed Local Leader produced a separate sustainability report. As stated by the continuous improvement consultant:

> We didn't have the conversations with key staff, with branches and with management around GRI reporting. We took that first step without actually having that engagement ... I think it's separate because we recognised last year – and I wasn't involved in last year's process – that we did need to have an engagement of staff. We needed to develop awareness, an understanding of the basics and the climate of sustainability reporting because I don't think they were as developed. We're beginning to do that here now and we're talking about across the organisation, not in a central area which is what probably occurred in the past. We had one full-time member who ran around and knocked on everyone's doors and said, 'Hey I need your data by this date for this report'. That was the level of dialogue.

Lack of integration of data for decision-making

Many respondents believed that sustainability data was not sufficiently integrated or used for decision-making. As stated by the continuous improvement consultant:

> We're looking at what it is [the sustainability data] that people actually use and I think that's got to be a primary driver in terms of understanding an organisation. There is no point collecting data that will never be used.

There is also a lack of integration among different divisions within the organisation structure, which undermines the usefulness of the information to the organisation as a whole. Lack of contribution from accountants was highlighted in some responses. The group accountant stated:

> As far as sustainability goes, I guess I certainly have had input into the year-end report that they were doing. I guess, to be perfectly fair ... I get frustrated with the report because it's really just lip-service to me. It's just, if we need to do a sustainability report do let's do it, and this is what we need to do. Let's just run around madly and get all the information that we need to put into this report now. You do that for maybe a month, get all the information, put it into the report and then it dies. It doesn't drive any process improvements or changes in thinking or anything like that. It's simply a report to go out to the public and say, this is what we're doing.

The manager, engineering services stated:

> For accountants ... I think you have a disconnect, for example: somebody who wants to maintain a road surface is basically going out there and looking at it from a technical element, without necessarily responding to the drivers for reporting. Most of that seems to occur at a managerial level, those drivers. They just push downwards and say, 'All right, we need a works program, we need this to be done,' and it's not necessarily embedded even at the tech officer level. Why are we doing this? We're doing this to keep the road going.

The strains and competing demands for time and resources between the IT and financial services division was also apparent in some of the responses. The group accountant stated:

> It is a trouble area because this group has got a huge workload – I mean everyone's just saying, 'I want this, I want this, I

want this' – so ultimately this group can't deliver their huge workload, they only deliver this [sustainability data]. They're no one's friends because they're not delivering what everyone wants because they just don't have the capacity to, essentially.

The lack of integration affects specific sustainability policies, such as the purchasing policy. The group accountant stated:

At the moment, what we're trying to do is in our tendering documents, when people go out to tender, which is over $100,000, make sure they've actually considered environmental issues. The environmental component has been there a long time, but we're just introducing the social component of it, which is really tough for people to actually think, 'Well, what should be the measure?' At the moment, we've got very bland things in there. Like, if we're procuring a service, we think about things like whether the organisation has an equal opportunities policy and stuff like that.

Political factors

Some respondents thought that Local Leader was more interested in political survival than in financial and non-financial information. The group accountant stated:

They don't care less. So they're interested in my political survival, so what can I do to get re-elected? Well, I can give lots of money to the community that will get me re-elected. So that's where their focus is on, making sure that there are services out there for the community.

The only way they're going to get interested in it [sustainability] is if it actually impacts their bonus. That's the only way that they would take an interest in it.

Little understanding of what constitutes sustainability

It was clear from many respondents that there was no clear framework or definition of sustainability within the organisation. The lack of clear parameters and boundaries creates confusion and ultimately inertia.

The manager, engineering services stated:

> A consultant was engaged to push forward what everybody thought defined sustainability and she came into these meetings with no definition at all. At the end of probably about three months of various sessions, I'm still not convinced that we had a defined place, but everybody understood just how big an animal it was. You could sort of touch it, but you didn't necessarily understand it.

The manager, financial services stated:

> When you get to the sustainability impacts, it's kind of like … that's a bit hard. There's no generally accepted framework of sustainability measures that we can use and say, 'Okay, it's this, this and this'. I mean carbon trading might be one of the ones that falls into that space.

> Sustainability as we're talking around this, it's not a simple thing; it's not a simple measure. You can't point to one thing and say, 'Well, that's the problem'. If it was simple, we'd all be doing it.

Lack of organisational support and clout

Another interesting theme to emerge from some respondents was a lack of organisation support and clout for sustainability information. This was surprising given Local Leader's strong public profile. As stated by the manager, financial services:

There are probably a few members on the council who are committed to some sort of sustainability, but that's limited. I mean there's only one councillor who's really raising the flag of sustainability on a regular basis; that's [name suppressed], but he's not going to stand for the next election, so there will be another green councillor possibly.

When questioned who supports sustainability within Local Leader, the manager, financial services stated:

City design, parts of engineering, definitely parts of our division. There are a couple of councillors, a couple of directors – but the thing is, and the good thing about this, is its growing. It's no longer a lone voice in the wilderness going back four or five years. Where now it is coming to the fore that people are starting to understand that it's here and it's here to stay, it's not going to go away. We are going to have to pursue it. One of the interesting things that are coming out now is that people are actually starting to look at one of the key things that they consider when they are looking at ... sustainability. If I go back to about three years ago, we used to have sustainability attachments on the reports. That's gone now because literally it was, we know what the answer is so we will just rework the inputs so we get to the right answer and it'll fall over the line. Now, they are starting to think about a lot of other things in terms of sustainability, particularly like the finance models that we work to. We are actually looking at it and going, 'Well, yes, I could do that two or three years ago but going forward the way I do things isn't sustainable'. You go, 'Why not?' 'Well, it just isn't, we can't keep doing what have done.'

A case study analysis of Clear Water

Background of Clear Water

Clear Water is controlled by the state government and is responsible for managing the water supply catchments for a capital city and to remove and treat most of the city's sewerage. Clear Water is also responsible for the treatment and supply of drinking water and recycled water for non-drinking purposes. Clear Water maintains drainage systems, rivers and creeks. In total Clear Water, manages approximately $8.4 billion in assets.

In its 2009–10 annual report Clear Water listed its key stakeholders as its 'customers, government, regulators, other water businesses, land developers, the community and suppliers'. Clear Water claims to approach its key business decisions by considering the short-term and long-term social, environmental and financial impacts of its activities. This is underscored by the organisation's ambitious goal of achieving zero net greenhouse gas emissions by 2018, principally by obtaining all its energy requirements from renewable sources and its clearly defined vision of ensuring a 'sustainable water future'. To realise this vision Clear Water defines seven business focus areas, where each focus area has particular goals assigned to them. These are outlined in the annual report as follows:

- Water resources:

  Manage water resources in a sustainable manner and secure supplies for a range of uses in the context of population growth and climate change.

- Public health:

  Protect public health by providing safe water, sewerage, and drainage services.

- Natural environment:

Protect, conserve, and improve natural assets and use natural resources sustainably.

- Built assets:
Plan, build and manage assets efficiently by adopting innovative solutions and whole-of-life approaches to meet customer service, community, and environmental objectives.
- Financial management:
Maintain financial viability and increase business value through effective and efficient financial and risk management.
- Our people and our workplace:
Foster a constructive work culture and safe workplace, where we achieve great results through collaboration, innovation and a commitment to excellence.
- External relationships:
Be recognised as a reliable and trustworthy organisation, willing to listen, work collaboratively and deliver on our promises.

These goals are closely aligned to key performance indicators (KPIs) outlined in the organisation's Corporate Plan and Water Plan, with the goal of embedding them deeply into the organisation's culture and *modus operandi*.

To help realise its vision for sustainability, Clear Water created a strategic framework, which was first established in 2006 and updated in 2008. This strategic framework set the backdrop for Clear Water's planning processes. These planning processes were established to ensure that social, environmental and economic impacts were considered across the matrix of the organisation's business operations and activities. Sustainability strategies are published in the three-year corporate plan, along with the corresponding performance measures and key performance indicators. The corporate plan is a three-year plan that is reviewed on an annual basis. The water plan, on the other hand, is a three to five-year action plan that sets out how to implement key strategies to achieve the desired sustainability outcomes, including revenue and tariff targets. The current water plan commenced in 2008 and runs until 2013. The strategic framework also plays an important role in linking Clear Water's efforts and strategies with those of the state government.

Regulatory environment of Clear Water

Clear Water is subject to extensive regulation to protect state water supplies, the environment and public health. Clear Water also administers specific legislation and related by-laws. The main purpose of this legislation is to promote the equitable and efficient use of water resources, ensure water resources are conserved and properly managed, and increase community involvement in conserving and managing water resources. There are also by-laws relating to protecting catchments and the water supply system, and preventing pollution of and damage to the catchments and water supply system. Other by-laws relate to preventing or minimising interference with the flow of water; preventing or minimising pollution of waterways and prohibiting or regulating the removal of materials from waterways.

Why Clear Water was selected for a case study

Clear Water was chosen for this research because of its reputation as an industry leader in the field of sustainability and because it is an organisation that recognises the impact of climate change on its core business. Although Clear Water is controlled by the state government, the organisation is governed by senior executives with a strong internal vision and focus on a sustainable water future. Clear Water has put a comprehensive strategic framework in place to ensure that the social, environmental and economic impacts of its activities are being considered on a day-to-day basis in its business operations. Not only is Clear Water working to ensure a sustainable water future, but the organisation has also committed to become a zero net greenhouse gas emitter by 2018.

Respondents selected for the case study

Respondents were drawn from a wide cross-section of the organisation. Twenty-two interviews were conducted, averaging approximately one hour each. Interviews were held with a number senior managers, divisional heads and professional staff, including a financial accountant, the sustainability planner, the team leader sustainability, corporate strategy, environmental management, team leader, information management, team leader, employee engagement and internal communications, the executive officer, office of the managing director, a senior health and safety adviser, the chairman of the board, manager, finance, the GM, comms and community relations, manager, corporate strategy, the GM, business services, sustainability coordinator, marketing manager, the energy and greenhouse manager, manager, HR services and the purchasing manager. Interviews were carried out over a two-year period, between 2006 and 2008. Some respondents, such as the manager of corporate strategy, were interviewed twice, while the environmental manager was interviewed three times over the sample period.

Outline of case study

The remainder of this case analysis is organised as follows.

Section one explores some of the issues surrounding the public image of sustainability projected by Clear Water and the perceptions of sustainability reporting by respondents working daily with the programs and initiatives within the organisation.

Section two explores Clear Water's processes, systems and methodologies for the collection, integration and reporting of sustainability information.

Section three explores the extent to which stakeholder engagement influences or impacts on sustainability reporting practices within the organisation.

Section four discusses potential hurdles confronting the collection, integration and reporting of sustainability information with the organisation.

Finally, some conclusions and policy implications are considered.

SECTION ONE

Public image versus internal perceptions

As an organisation, Clear Water realised early in the last decade that its position in relation to becoming 'sustainable' was precarious and there was a fundamental need for cultural renewal. There appeared to be a deep sense of realisation within the organisation that if Clear Water's internal commitment to sustainability was not a genuine one, the public would recognise that. Various sustainability initiatives, policies and practices were set in motion by the organisation's senior leadership that eventually led to the more visible culture of sustainability we see today.

The chairman of the board recollected the somewhat perilous position of Clear Water in relation to sustainability, which provided impetus for the development of a comprehensive sustainability framework which drives the organisation today, stating:

> We had just had the report that Clear Water had commissioned – I did a report into climate change – modelling the catchment with the CSIRO model and it clearly showed that as of early 2004, climate change was going to have a big impact on this business. The organisation had also joined the Greenhouse Challenge back in 2002 ... at that point we were in the top 15 energy users in the state and climate change was a result of coal-fired energy and so it was like a vicious circle for us, an absolute vicious circle.
>
> I mean if you look at climate change, the water industry is the most affected. If you regard it as an industry, the water yield is the most affected and so I had to say we were contributing significantly to our downfall. So I said, 'Look, on that basis, I think we should have a sustainability framework which

should sit above the corporate plan and should sit above the regulator – it should sit above that and it should drive behaviours in the organisation', and that [report into climate change] was the result of that.

The report was developed initially with a board leadership team focus and then throughout the organisation and throughout our stakeholders. It was a mechanism to engage our organisation in a cultural renewal. And the frog which I still wear every day has become a symbol of change in the organisation, and change about sustainability. Recently, the PowerPoint master sheet was changed and the frog dropped off and there was outrage in the organisation because the frog represents the focus on sustainability in this organisation. That is everything we do. We have to think about the future because the other aspect of it is that we manage the waterways. Quite unusually; we act as a catchment management authority. On one hand we take water out of them and on the other hand we actually manage their health.

To effect such wide-sweeping cultural renewal, a commitment to sustainability had to come from the highest level of the organisation, particularly the board level. The then chairman of the board stated:

Whether it's the science, or whether it's the lawyer, or whether it's the accountant, or the engineers, we actually have to change the way we do business and if we can't make this work, nobody will make it work because it actually does fundamentally, more than any other business I have ever been in, actually threaten the business completely.

The board of directors played a critical leadership role in sustainability, particularly in tackling bureaucrats, policymakers and accountants in the government itself. The chairman of the board said:

> So this is an ongoing fight, an ongoing battle. Of course the policymakers will say we want you to be sustainable. What does that really mean? And the best example form is mini hydros. We fitted six and we've got eight more – 14 altogether – which we have evaluated as prime sites. The reason we have fitted six is that they all have positive net present value, even marginally. The last few that were marginal resulted in terrible arguments from Treasury, along the lines of 'This is not in your core business, why would you be doing this?' So we go back to these principles, we go back to our obligations as stated by government.

These obligations included inculcation of sustainability principles within the organisation, which the board fought to include in its formal planning and strategy. This process did not always go smoothly as the government itself appeared to only provide 'motherhood principle' support for sustainability, and not real sustainability obligations. The chairman of the board said:

> The government has given us a statement of obligations – what our obligations are to government – and I have worked very hard to have sustainability in a meaningful way within the first round. I thought in the second round we had got it in there in a more meaningful way, but it has been two years of work and, at the very last minute without consultation, it has been dismantled ... it is still there. It is still supported in the motherhood way. I really wanted it to be there in a way that put an obligation on us to operate in a sustainable way. That meant more than just a motherhood principle.

In various interviews, there appeared to be a particularly strong commitment to various sustainability policies and the development of particular sustainability processes, programs, plans and initiatives. Internally, respondents appeared seriously committed and engaged in creating and following policies that had a 'real impact' on the organisation, as opposed to green-sounding public relations campaigns aimed at improving the outward image of Clear Water. This attitude appeared to filter down from the board to various middle managers within the organisation. For instance, the team leader sustainability and corporate strategy said:

> Before I even started, the board had developed the strategic framework ... it was developed before I even started. This isn't the whole thing, but this is essentially the structure of it. We had our sustainability principles and these are our priority areas and goals. We brought it back to what's important for our business, and what are the areas under that, and how do we need to sort of develop sustainability further along that. Now, this isn't perfect and I think if I had been involved with the process, there might have been a few little things. I think there are some overarching issues that probably aren't picked up as well. But I think, overall, it's actually very good and it was developed by the board. It was their first go at doing this [developing strategic framework] and ensuring sustainability principles underpinned it and I think it's a pretty good go. So that was kind of already there. That was the board doing that ... our MD was doing a bit of a road show ... he went around and did about 20 or 30 little individual sessions of just 15 people at each session – 15 to 20 at each session – depending on whether it was at one of the outside sites or was in here in one of the meeting rooms. He just went through this whole thing and went through the way the board was directing the

organisation and what the priorities were. He went through the fact that sustainability is a priority for us.

Now, the other side of it is, there has been this preferred culture. We have a preferred culture model which is the OCI – the Organisational Culture Index – and it's this thing that shows whether you're blue, green or red in an organisation. So we went through that, before I started, as an organisation and then each individual group went through it to see how their groups functioned or how their groups rated and then we had to do it at general manager level and then the next direct reports down. Well, I'm the next level down from that and, about six months after I started, I did it as well. So all of us at that level have an understanding of where we are personally, but we also understand where the organisation is as well. So the idea was to move towards this blue culture.

There appeared to be a strong commitment to sustainability across the organisation, particularly among younger employees. The team leader of sustainability and corporate strategy also stated:

I have been amazed at how on-board people are with the sustainability concept and understanding that we manage a natural resource. We provide public health services and understand that there are issues there that we need to manage, and we try to manage them very well. We have a pretty good culture and a lot of people in their 20s and 30s who are just full of ideas and just amazing. They're different to some of the engineers in their 50s and 60s, who have always done things and that's probably one of the things you are overcoming as well. That's actually not a really big hurdle, I think. There's enough of a momentum being developed now, and I guess that's part of my role and our team, being part of that momentum.

The importance of sustainability is emphasised at the organisation level, but Clear Water also implements programs to engender a sustainability-oriented attitude within the daily lives of its employees. The team leader sustainability and corporate strategy stated:

> We're doing it at a number of different levels. I guess our main one for organisational culture change is the Living Smart Program. That's a program that is supposed to give people understanding that there are things here that you can be doing, but ... [also that] there are things you can be doing everywhere in your life. So it's not about just what you do at work, it's not about what you might just do at home and leave when you come to work, it's about your whole focus on life. So we educate people on issues and we encourage them and we promote and we do lots of different things to do that, and we bring it back to how it's relevant to their every day job, because we think that's important. We also bring it back to what they can do in their home and why it's important for them in their everyday lives as well. So that's probably our biggest ongoing initiative, to facilitate that culture change.

Some respondents believed sustainability was having more of an impact at the 'big picture' level (in terms of big decisions about big projects) but less at the day-to-day business level. As stated by the marketing manager:

> Yeah, I think we've been – without being cute – on this journey to really incorporate sustainability into our day-to-day thinking. We've had quite a lot of discussions lately around, you know, the business thinks that way now. In terms of making big decisions about big projects, that works really well at that level. I think there is still some work to be done in terms of people thinking of sustainability in the way

they go about their day-to-day business. I know I've found it challenging myself because ... I've had to start using it in my own day-to-day practice and it's a lot of effort and I've got to change my way of doing things. But I think that's important, you've got to start doing that if you're going to be practising what you're preaching.

Respondent interviews suggested that the internal perception of sustainability and its interpretation for the organisation as a whole was becoming a significant part of Clear Water's culture, permeating all levels of the organisation. This appears to be reflected in how Clear Water presents its image to the public. An example of this was the approach taken in preparing Clear Water's sustainability report in 2008, at the time the interviews were held. A member of environmental management stated the organisation was not interested in a 'hollow' compliance with GRI indicators, saying:

That's why we don't do it in accordance with [the GRI]. The other issue is that the GRI is coming out at the wrong end. They're sort of saying, 'Here's a reporting method that will make you a really good sustainable organisation'. We don't want to do it that way. We want to say, 'Why do we want to be a sustainability organisation?' And then we'll do that and then the reporting will flow out, which is much more proper.

While it was evident that Clear Water had not settled on the best approach for reporting sustainability information, the organisation appeared to actively strive to create a comprehensive report that its stakeholders could understand. An example of this is how Clear Water continually reassessed how it reported on sustainability, particularly in terms of integrating and aligning sustainability information across the different products and activities of the organisation. The sustainability coordinator stated:

> For the first time, there's a lot more alignment between our water plan, our corporate plan and our sustainability report. So we did it [sustainability report] by product group this year: water, sewerage, waterways, recycled water, protecting our natural environment, our relationships, our people, our workplace and our business. It kind of half links into the strategic framework and half links into the corporate plan. It's a lot more aligned. The reason that we did that was the overwhelming response that people were finding it difficult to find the information they needed, because last year it was under the triple bottom line – social, environment[al], economic. So they're the two big changes this year.

While Clear Water does not follow a formal TBL reporting approach or methodology, the organisation appears to incorporate a TBL mentality into its day-to-day business operations and reporting. The GM, business services stated:

> In terms of how people talk about it [the sustainability report], they think environmental sustainability and there is certainly a focus on that but it is, for us, also around social sustainability in terms of community relations and stakeholder relations and the impact on the broader community. It's also about financial sustainability. That is to say you don't get to invest in maintaining or improving business performance unless you're making a dollar.

These elements of sustainability have their own KPIs at different levels within the organisation, allowing benchmarks to be set and reported on. They are ultimately used to drive improved performance within each category. The GM, business services said:

In terms of the greener side of sustainability, and social and financial actually, our performance plans individually and collectively for the management group do have targets within them, sometimes around particular projects that support the various aspects of sustainability. Depending on what level you are at, higher level KPIs are set, such as did we meet our financial targets? Did we meet our greenhouse energy target? Did we meet our community satisfaction target? So they are within our performance planning and reward and recognition frameworks.

Clear Water also appears to strive towards a higher level of transparency and accountability as part of its sustainability culture, even when this is potentially to the detriment of its public image. The chairman of the board discussed the organisation's attitude to reporting 'bad news' events, stating:

One of the other important things, and this doesn't necessarily go to your numeracy but in terms of reporting, is reporting the bad news as well. So I was around when Western Mining was the first to report negative news in their annual report. I think it was a breach of the dam wall at Olympic Dam, so a very serious one, and it wasn't known before the report was released. I listened to the debate around that positive and negative and, at the end of the day; I saw it as being incredibly positive about transparency. Part of this is about transparency and accountability too and I think that's a core value in sustainability ... we did something brave in this last year and I was very much part of the debate. [In our report] we declared two major environmental spills, which the EPA had not declared. One just happened in the month of June 2006 so at that time we had never been prosecuted before.

But these were both serious incidents and ... I think they were indicators of a systemic problem and they were. It did turn out to be a systemic problem; completely different sites.

However, the chairman of the board noted that higher level of transparency was rewarded almost immediately with a more positive result to something that could have turned into a public relations nightmare. The chairman of the board stated:

I fought very hard to have these [incidents] reported in that I believe that transparency and accountability are very much part of sustainability. So we put them in and only last Wednesday we went to court – the Magistrates Court – and we were actually not convicted, but we pleaded guilty and we would always have to plead guilty because it is strict liabilities that happen from our sites; there is no defence. We received a $150,000 fine across both – it is a huge fine and again we expected that, it was very much a part of what we discussed with the EPA. We had worked very closely with the EPA and, in fact, developed a system of risk management for third-line maintenance areas, which EPA says is world class. And part of our penalty is to go out and talk to industry about this – Australian industry groups like plastics and chemicals industries. But the fact is it was in there. It was certainly waived in court and I think that their barrister [EPA's] used the fact that we had not completely disclosed – because there were some things that we didn't actually know in June at the time we printed – nevertheless, it actually totally assisted in the fact that there was no story because it had already been disclosed. We will disclose it again notwithstanding the fact that there may be a prosecution to that.

SECTION TWO

Sustainability: data collection, measurement and reporting

It was clear from the interviews that Clear Water faced several challenges in developing data collection, measurement and reporting processes necessary for producing its sustainability report. There are many different professionals, contractors, departments and various business areas that create, collect and manage a large amount of sustainability data and information. The respondents indicated that often the exchange among different business teams and divisions does not occur, as described by the chairman of the board:

> Very good examples are in the drainage and planning teams, fabulous data, but they do not talk to each other. They don't talk to the waterways team even, let alone their science and research team, let alone the accounting teams.

The chairman of the board pointed out substantive measurement and integration problems with sustainability data, stating:

> We do measure all of the compliance things, but we are beginning to measure some of the other things. It's always an issue of who collects the data. It is not collected from the accounting team, it's collected from the sustainability team, which is in the research in the science team ... I mean everybody collects data in little pockets all over the organisation.

Accountants appear to have the most difficulty with the measurement of sustainability information. This is reflected in some of the attitudes expressed by the chairman of the board who believes the accounting profession needs to take more direct leadership and responsibility in the sustainability field:

> I should start out by saying I, for, some time, have been saying that until we get the accountancy profession to pick up this as an accounting responsibility then we won't move forward. So this goes back to, I think, the last review into environmental accounting.

However, the accounting departments are not the only sections of Clear Water that create various information exchange and communication challenges. There are many departments and localised sections within Clear Water that have created their own data silos, which can limit the effective integration of sustainability information and reduce its accessibility across the organisation. The environmental manager stated:

> I think the silos have to be looked at to become serviceable, so that people can actually use them and get stuff out of them instead of just putting the data in, and there are a few organisational paths that do that. The data is just going in and that's it because you need to use it. Our waterway quality database is a bit like that I think.

Often these 'pockets' of information are managed by highly skilled individuals that have created them for specific localised tasks. While the information has broader applications across the organisation, the information cannot be readily accessed to be useful in the reporting process. The GM of business services stated:

> Clear Water has been pretty blessed with a lot of very technically skilled people that have developed their own little systems ... some of those systems are still going – like those related to our water quality, our flow monitoring and

flow prediction and rainfall prediction ... all that. We still have some local databases and local systems that we are progressively working through to make sure there is good governance from a data management perspective, but also rolling those through – you know thinking about it in the context of getting a broader number of people access to that data. So there is still some work in progress on it from a number of our key technical gurus.

The team leader of information management described one example of these 'data silos' in the context of the newly implemented SCADA[1] system:

A new SCADA system went in and we've created a master database, which we've called Waterworks, which is managing things like billing water and we're going to be billing sewerage etc. and ... it's going to be using the data that comes out of the SCADA system to do a whole range of functions to do with planning and billing and a whole range of things.

The predominant initiative mentioned by respondents to tackle this issue is the introduction of a data warehouse, as the GM, business services described it:

The data warehouse has increasingly become an important part of our overall business reporting, including a range of our targets, be they financial, operational, I think also in terms of picking up the sustainability targets. We battled with the concept of a data warehouse for a few years, the cost, we thought, did not make the concept appear beneficial.

---

1 SCADA (Supervisory Control and Data Acquisition) is a system that collects data from various sensors at remote locations and sends this data to a central computer that then manages and controls the data.

I think, ultimately, the need for us to respond more quickly to outside stakeholders like the Essential Services Commission and others meant that we needed to put in place better systems and governance arrangements around our KPI reporting. So there are a few stages to the data warehouse. We are currently working on stage two, but that is really a critical part of making sure we get consistent, timely information on a range of our performance indicators and not just for annual reports. I mean the KPIs that we manage, but also a range of other operational KPIs that help our business managers manage day-to-day.

So the data warehouse has become an increasingly important part of our overall business reporting and business management and it picks up a range of KPIs. In terms of some of the sustainability ones, like greenhouse gases and others, it's picking up those as well. You might have seen some information as you walked in on some more of our internal paper use targets. That information is still very manually developed and hopefully, in the next round of the data warehouse, we will put in place processes where the system just spits it out and we spend more time managing the issue rather than gathering the data on the issue. I think at the moment it's probably being used more at the higher level, that's true. I think going forward we will need to use it at a more operational level.

So our first response I think is around being able to respond to the ESC and external stakeholders so that helps, giving them confidence that the data is consistent, good governance ... so that's the first stage of it. The next response is probably translating the information to our Board, but as the data warehouse goes into its next stages, people who manage different business processes within our business need to be aware of the performance of them. I'm confident, and it is, for me, necessary, that it will become part of the day-to-day management tools that people have to get a quick snapshot of where things are at. It's not the only place, you know, we will report on how things are going. We have SCADA systems and we have an IT system, we have got a screen up there that tells us whether the system is running slow, quick or somewhere in between. So we have other systems that help us with the day-to-day monitoring but in terms of measures of final outputs of what we are here to do, the data warehouse is becoming increasingly important ... it sucks the information out of the operating system. So it's not just someone encoding the data into a data warehouse, some of that happens because we have still got to improve some of the integration between the systems but progressively it's dragging the information out of the finance system, out of the asset management system – if not, it will be dragging the data out of our SCADA system. So it is integrating the information out of those systems into a user-friendly form so to speak, simplifying it.

While the data warehouse is envisaged to become a very powerful tool in the way sustainability information can be compiled, disseminated, managed and reported on, there are still major integration hurdles to overcome. The team leader of information management stated:

One of the key things at the moment is just the logic of who built the telemetry system, the SCADA system, we're actually working on something as basic as [generic software export] drivers so we can spit the data out from their data sources into Sequel databases and be able to use it in our data warehouse, interrogate it through normal Sequel processes, that sort of stuff. So there's some interesting stuff going on but as always it's a matter of just trying to round up. It's herding cats basically.

Respondents indicated that IT technicians, with the support of the business areas they service, have been striving to build more integrated systems to support the information gathering process for the sustainability report. The team leader of information management noted some progress with the integration of sustainability information:

One [area of progress] is the project that we're doing in Waterways where we're trying to develop authoritative sources of information and well entrenched architectures that provide functionality while rounding up the information so that it can be validated and reported on. Secondary to that is that once we've got reliable sources of data that are supporting the business processes, and then we can have the KPI management system and data warehouse to manipulate the data. I think we're in a far stronger position to be able to do that sort of thing now than we were a couple of years ago. It's taken a fair bit of time. It's all fairly time-intensive because a lot of it is about those definitions or process analysis exercises as much as anything else, and has taken a lot of commitment from the business. There has probably been just as much commitment from the business to providing resources and people and time etc. as there has been from the IT department, and a lot of it has been creating a good working relationship between the guys in IT and the guys in the business.

The chairman of the board observed that in terms of sustainability data and information there needs to be a distinction drawn between financial and non-financial information, which will be handled differently in terms of any integration exercise, stating:

> Where we can actually gain numbers [on sustainability], I think they need to go into things like the data warehouse so that we can access them. Where there are things that are more non-numeric then they will come out of the sustainability team, like where it relies on a survey, for instance. Even though a physical copy of a survey may have all the data, the data still needs to be logged. But when that survey says, for example, total water discharge and quality, that needs to go into the data warehouse. It might be collected from five or six or seven or eight sites or more, but it needs to go into data warehouse.

Even with financial data, some respondents noted there were major problems confronting the effective integration of information sources with data warehouse. The manager of finance was pessimistic about the value of the entire data warehouse exercise:

> I'm not that familiar with the data warehouse. I know that it's supposed to be like we've got this key performance indicator report that goes to the board. It's supposed to all be driven by the data warehouse. All I can tell you from the whinges I've heard in the first month from my team is that it didn't work as seen and we're having difficulty with people taking ownership and putting in their data. Finance is seen as the ultimate people that produce the KPI report, so I know last month, to get that report out, it all fell back to finance ringing around and getting the numbers. It hasn't worked that well, yet. I won't say it won't.

The chairman of the board was more adamant about the need to align sustainability information more closely with the financial reporting process, and more particularly for the accounting profession to take an active role in the process:

> So I actually think this belongs with the accounting team and I think it belongs with a single audit process ... but I should start out by saying, I for some time have been saying that until we get the accountancy profession to pick up this as an accounting responsibility then we won't move forward. There is only one way it can be done and that is to line it up with our financial reporting process.

According to the chairman of the board this could have happened more readily:

> [If the accountancy profession] had they come on board ten years ago, they would have started measuring the things we can measure, for example the output in a waste product. So, if you go out and have a look in your bin, what's in there, and we would have actually had some numbers around the things that we can measure or we would have taken a leap. We have to start documenting and reporting the things that we can measure before we actually go into the next thing. How do we measure things like fugitive emissions?

Global Reporting Index

Clear Water only uses the GRI in a limited way for sustainability reporting purposes. Several respondents indicated that many GRI indicators are not appropriate for an organisation such as Clear Water. Many other indicators have been internally generated by Clear Water to reflect the organisation's sustainability profile in a more meaningful way. The sustainability coordinator stated:

Look, I think the GRI is useful in terms of having an international benchmark but it's not the be all and end all for what Clear Water is doing. It's just something else that adds in to the pot. I also think that the process that the GRI suggests is an interesting one for the sustainability report. But it's still seen as a separate process.

Respondents suggested that Clear Water's goal is to become a sustainable organisation first and then create the appropriate reporting framework around it, while the GRI prescribes a way of reporting that leads to a sustainable organisation. A member of the environmental management team stated:

That's what the GRI is trying to do. They're saying to everybody in the world, 'Do this and you won't be killing people in Africa and you won't be using child labour, and you won't be polluting the waterways and you will therefore be a much more sustainable organisation'. Whereas we're saying we want to be a sustainable organisation anyway and we'll work that out ourselves what that means and then we'll report on it.

The marketing manager suggested that the GRI is an important guide but Clear Water needs to develop its own indicators as well as adapting others, saying:

There was a lot of discussion at the start to say there are these indicators, do we have to use those? Some of them aren't relevant to an organisation like ours and do we have the capability to be able to pick and choose which ones suit what we are about? Then we thought we'd maybe look at some other indicators like those of the Australian Water Association. I think they developed those as ones more relevant to the water industry, saying, 'Let's choose which of the GRI are most appropriate and maybe look at some other indicators'.

SECTION THREE

Stakeholder engagement

It was evident from several respondents that Clear Water strongly perceives itself as a stakeholder-focused organisation. In its strategic framework Clear Water identified four areas vital to achieving its organisational vision, namely:

- its challenges
- its business areas
- its culture
- its stakeholders.

Clear Water's vision, as stated in its 2009–10 report, is, 'Working together to ensure a sustainable water future' and under the heading of 'delivering our vision' the strategic framework directly aligns its vision with stakeholders.

External stakeholders

In general, Clear Water's engagement with its external stakeholders appears to have both breadth and depth. Many respondents appeared particularly cognisant that the organisation has a unique impact on local communities and the environment; which has led to a cultural and strategic focus on adopting 'best practices', as well as actively engendering bilateral communications and dialogue with the community. The GM of business services stated:

> We judge ourselves – well, we try to adopt best practice around corporate governance principles and in a range of ways do a lot of good work with the community in an operational sense and then engaging with the community through surveys and the like to understand what the community's needs are and

how we respond to them. So, communication is absolutely vital to the success of our businesses.

The GM of business services was keenly aware of how profoundly external stakeholders can impact the organisation, particularly in areas such as water quality:

> How our stakeholders view us, how the community views us in terms of their confidence in our ability to deliver, some of that's around the fact that we are so passionate around water quality in our business and, I know we have the retailers as part of the model, but we reinforce our passion for working with government to maintain our protected catchments, to keep water quality at the highest level ... at the end of the day, you are judged by the quality of the water that comes through the pipes, so if we lose credibility in that in whatever sense probably the rest of our business is stuffed as well.

Clear Water appears to actively seek out what stakeholders want and seems keenly aware on how its actions are perceived. At least at the board level, transparency is perceived as much a part of sustainability as accountability. As stated previously, the chairman of the board alluded to the fact that the organisation reported to stakeholders on both the successes and failings of the organisation, even against legal advice.

The focus on stakeholder transparency was also emphasised by the manager of corporate strategy:

> Okay, well, we define sustainability very broadly as an organisation. I guess you are aware [of that]. So therefore that comment about, you know, what are you going to release and what you are not ... I think the fact that the board has interpreted sustainability broadly and the fact that we are

a public organisation and we are looking to be transparent as required under the GRI, then put as much information in as we think ... but it has got to be readable. You want to encourage people to actually sit down [and read it].

The Chief Financial Officer stated the importance of understandable, readable sustainability information to stakeholders:

Having these debates about putting in the value of water, it's meaningless, I reckon. And that's where hopefully this TBL stuff will come in. Something that will move forward as a profession in the community will be to recognise the people that this ultimately goes to, and to help them understand it. And by putting in convoluted theories and formulas and all sorts of stuff, yes, we all pat ourselves on the back, but this will end up being 400 pages and no one will read it.

When dealing with its suppliers and contractors, Clear Water actively pursues sustainability orientated policies. The GM of business services stated that Clear Water seeks to establish lasting relationships with its suppliers and contractors but has an active policy of sustainable procurement, saying:

We look to develop strong relationships with our constructors and our suppliers with an emphasis on sustainable procurement, and that has seen initiatives like our sludge drying pans, not the use of clay but the use of recycled concrete. When we picked our contractors, we looked at their approach to procurement, their environmental practices, their health and safety practices, their approach to dealing with the community. So, in our contracts and our procurement philosophies ... we would not work with an environmental vandal ... health and safety, well we're not going to work with someone who hurts people and we are going to continue with the people who can bring sustainable philosophies to our business. So we try and work in partnership with all our suppliers on all those different aspects. Just back on the environmental vandal stuff, we were looking at a building a while ago before we came here and one of the oil companies [had a few floors on it], I forget which one it was – but even if they were good we thought, well, it's not good for a water business to be seen in a building with an oil company.

One good example of Clear Water's sustainable procurement focus was in recycled concrete. The GM of business services stated:

We are encouraging industry – the construction industry – to come up with different solutions and a really significant one is the use of recycled concrete in our pans, which is nothing environmentally fantastic, but in terms of asset management performance, it's brilliant compared to clay which, when they harvest the sludge, it is a bit soft and going to get torn up. The concrete has a longer life so it's a better environmental outcome and better financial outcome because we don't have to replace the clay liner as much.

However, more often than not the ultimate effectiveness of Clear Water's sustainable procurement policy was not clear-cut; particularly during a tendering process where Clear Water is faced with trade-offs between the social, environmental and the economic aspects of each procurement. The purchasing manager said:

We do have a triple bottom line assessment ... so yes, the environment can be taken into consideration, so basically it will be to input a cost dollar figure on it. Often we can't, so then we have to use some other kind of measure and then a weighting to that measure compared to price.

The purchasing manager discussed another initiative that underscored Clear Water's sustainability oriented purchasing policy. This was the addition of a sustainability drop-down menu to act as a reminder of what ought to be considered in every purchase transaction:

> Then our finance system was being upgraded and [we thought,] is there anything we can do there? So we actually put it on our system that next to the requisition, when you're making a requisition, there's a box – just a sustainable question mark. If you drop down the list, it brings up the different categories that relate back to our sustainable policy – reduce waste and save energy and that sort of thing.

Another major stakeholder of Clear Water is the commission,[2] which regulates the prices and service standards for the provision of water and sewerage services. Clear Water is dependent on the commission's regulatory approval for its water plan which, in turn, will affect its major revenue streams. In order to raise enough money to support its sustainability policies, Clear Water needs to convince the regulator of their efficiency. The manager of business strategy described the process as follows:

> I don't know if you are aware of what regulated businesses have to do to get their money, but it basically means [you have to] front the regulator and put up a good case. So, for the last water plan, we put up five years' worth of substantial proposals around sustainability and I think we were helped

---

2 The state government established an independent economic regulator of essential services.

enormously this time by the fact that ... we now have a sustainability clause in there which says we have to do things according to sustainability principles, we have to set up programs to do X, Y and Z. That had a direct link to, I guess, dealing with the impacts of climate change. So we then went out and did some work with the community and the community are hugely supportive about us spending money on, you know, renewable energy and greenhouse reductions. That has helped our business.

Internal stakeholders

Clear Water sees its internal stakeholders as primarily employees and the state government as the controlling shareholder. For example, with regard to reducing greenhouse gas and improving renewable energy, Clear Water carried out numerous sustainability activities and implemented a number of organisational changes. Initially the strategies implemented also made financial sense, they were net present value (NPV) positive and thus it was not too difficult to engender support from the government. Some respondents commented that while the government likes to wear the 'green hat' in public, it is driven predominantly by financial interests. More recent sustainability initiatives were less commercially viable even though they made sense from a sustainability perspective. Hence, it became increasingly difficult for Clear Water to secure financial support for some of its sustainability initiatives, resulting in more resources being spent by the organisation in convincing the government of the value of the initiatives.

These conflicts are captured by the manager of corporate strategy:

So we were getting to the stage where we were thinking, 'How are we going to get this through Treasury?' Ultimately, they are most concerned about the almighty dollar. You know you can spin them all sorts of lines around sustainability but, if the numbers don't stack up, you don't get things through ... well, you do but they have been skirmishes, rather than battles. So it is around the edges where we can improve our game.

So that's one change to the program, but the other change I think on energy was the fact that we had done great things in reducing greenhouse gas and improving renewable energy since 2000–01 and, as I said, we were sort of coming towards the end of the obvious commercial solutions and most of these were, you know, they were – if you made the investment you got a good pay back within a reasonable time. So, for the last set of mini hydros – I don't know whether you are aware of these things but we embed them, we are embedding them in the transfer system because we have got excess pressure really – one of them actually wasn't NPV positive and of course that's exactly where Treasury went to us and sort of said, 'What you are doing with this?' So, anyway, we managed to get them through on the basis that collectively they were [NPV positive], but I think they sent up a little bit of a warning sign to say, 'Don't send too many of these NPV negative ones to us'.

One of the most important things Clear Water did to engender sustainability engagement among its employees was to put the 'right people' in top level management positions. The chairman of the board stated:

Importantly, recruiting a CEO that has the same values, and where you develop that vision together, you recruit on the basis of the values. You develop the vision together with the entire organisation so that [now] we've got unbelievable buy-in in this organisation.

This allowed for a pervasive cultural change program to be implemented as described by the chairman of the board: 'Everyone talks about the blue culture in the organisation as opposed to the red and the green. So it is pervasive and it is about sharing and working together.' The manager of corporate strategy stated:

> There [are] the three colours and we refer to the blue colours as the blue culture and that talks about four particular attributes: achievement, self-actualisation, affiliation and another one's sort of like coaching and mentoring other people. And that's the part that we think will lead to improved business performance, whereas the red is more an aggressive type of culture and the green is a bit like hand balling, where you sort of look for ways to actually dodge it, pass it on, whatever.

Another example of the way this 'top down' engagement worked in the organisation is through KPIs, which the board adopts annually. The manager of corporate strategy said:

> The board ha[s] to each year adopt KPIs. And we've expanded the KPIs to include quite a lot of sustainability specific KPIs. I suppose the most important ones were the energy and greenhouse. But we've also now got KPIs around how we benchmark internationally on sustainability through the Dow Jones index. How we go office-wise on water, energy, paper and waste, how we go in terms of doing something on biodiversity and we're sort of surveying and developing management plans and implementing those for key buyer sites on our own land and so forth.

On the other side of the spectrum these KPIs are distributed across all employment levels to the point where notices are put up throughout the entire building to remind people and raise their awareness of the KPIs. The chairman of the board said, 'You probably noticed at the lifts on the way up ... we are setting some new KPIs in this area', while the manager of corporate strategy said, 'If you go to the toilet it will actually show the KPI results on water, waste and energy'.

Arguably, one of the most effective ways of engendering change through sustainability KPIs was linking certain performance objectives directly to bonuses. The sustainability coordinator stated:

> Paper is included in the Enterprise Agreement (EA) for this year, maybe next year. The EA's just been signed, so everyone's bonuses are based on that target being achieved, or a reduction in paper use being achieved. [The KPIs will be based on] paper in the first year, water and energy in the second year, and waste in the third year.

SECTION FOUR

Hurdles facing the collection, integration and reporting of sustainability information

The main hurdles facing the effective collection, integration and reporting of sustainability information within the organisation are the many isolated data centres, which do not communicate with each other. The chairman of the board said that this problem was largely a result of previous cultural attitudes fostered within Clear Water:

> This is about the culture. It goes right back to the beginning and it's about if you have an organisation where you drive competition and competitive behaviour and you are rewarded on that – then power is everything and data is power. So you don't let anybody let yourself get attacked. I am not kidding when I say that in this organisation, decisions were made at the very top of the organisation – and I don't mean the Board because they weren't regarded as the top of the organisation – and data was power. So it was very important in the old culture not to share.

The chairman of the board also said:

> The whole cultural change here is about getting people to work together as opposed to those old siloed areas. To do that, people need feedback and so they will need to get it from somewhere and, as it's cross-organisational, you will only get it from that sort of data warehouse type concept.

Another problem emanating from having too many different data sources is that there are just as many interpretations of them, which diminish their authority, making it difficult to decide which to use as benchmarks and in the reporting process. The manager of corporate strategy said:

> In the past you could get as many different answers as you could find people to ask. But in terms of authoritative, secure information, there wasn't any. So the idea of the data warehouse was simply to have exactly that – something that was secure, something that was the authority so you would only ever get one answer. A lot of this information was being kept on spread sheets, which is why you could always get different answers from different people.

The issue of too many data silos is exacerbated by a certain level of protectionism, specifically when one system like the data warehouse is threatening to undermine the authority from a localised system and the individual/s responsible for that system. This creates a culture of defensiveness. The sustainability coordinator said:

> Whenever I've asked people for information they've very freely given it to me and actually been pleased that it's being used for something and are quite proud that it makes it to the sustainability report. My job [involved] just getting information whereas [the team leader of information management] was trying to put a new system on top and I think people felt quite defensive about what was going to happen to their job and their position.

Furthermore the GM of business services said:

> If there are any barriers to improvement it will be around people issues. About people not wanting to share information, people saying 'this is what I do' – but I have got to say again they are in the minority.

On another front, Clear Water appears to be making progress in extracting the information needed for its strategic framework and KPIs in its periodic reports. However, the GM of business services observed there was still some way to go in getting the right data to allow better reporting on day-to-day operational information. The GM of business services said:

> I think we probably do need to, at a more operational level, look to see how we can bring together the different aspects of our finance system, energy costs and whatever system it is that shows you how much electricity you are using at a point in time. We have some elements of that but I reckon it's those areas where more detailed, in the moment, business information/reporting is needed. The period reporting stuff I think is pretty fine. I think it's probably more in the day-to-day decision-making stuff where we need to [improve].

Another hurdle to effective data collection and integration at the organisational level is the sheer size of Clear Water and its diversity of site locations and employees from different educational, professional and experience backgrounds. It was relatively straightforward to reach people at the head office but once outside this domain the site environments can change dramatically from site to site. The manager of corporate strategy stated:

> I think one of the issues is that it is a very diverse organisation … there are three hundred and something people here, sure, but there are a hell of a lot of people that are out there and they are working in roles like our treatment plants and water supply depots and so forth. To reach those people and to switch everybody on, sometimes you need to re-jig the message a bit and I think sometimes you need to convey the message in a different way. People don't necessarily react well

to emails. Quite often the face-to-face, and in the vernacular that they are used to, is a much better way of going.

There are also some trade-off issues in data collection. For instance, when considering data collection, do you hire an additional employee to collect the extra data, assign the task to an existing employee who then has less time for their original task, or get the information from an outside source? In the case of getting data from an outside source, a concern was raised by respondents as to whether or not that data would be verified. If it was not verified then it would not fall under the existing audit program of Clear Water. Environmental management said, 'If it's not checked, it's not audited and it's not ours. That's not a good way to go ... the data point wouldn't be checked'.

Another problem faced by Clear Water is the lack of adequate accounting standards and practices to guide the reporting of sustainability information, making it more difficult to effectively integrate sustainability data with financial information. A member of environmental management stated:

> It's [reporting of sustainability information] an accounting issue, and it's not dollars but it's accounting dollars because we had to spend 300 odd thousand dollars to make our renewable energy target last year, so it's coming in. Also, we gave away a lot of land to the government that we'd bought because we didn't need it, surplus land. We retained the native vegetation credits for that land, so we didn't have the land any more, but we had that asset, which was an additional asset to the value to the land, because the government introduced their net gain system. So somebody out there had to chop some trees down and they couldn't find any offset, so they bought them off us. So we made [amount suppressed] out of that transaction, but we don't know how to account for those things.

A case study analysis of Infrastructor

Background of Infrastructor

Infrastructor currently has operating divisions delivering services across a diverse range of fields including mining, civil, building, process, rail, services and tunnelling.

Infrastructor brings detailed knowledge of successful construction process and has a strong collaborative culture with clients, particularly in terms of:

- providing strategic procurement models
- integrating with client processes
- developing relationships with key suppliers
- delivering cost-effective solutions.

Infrastructor is one of the world's largest suppliers of outsourced mining services. Worldwide, Infrastructor mines more than 67 million tonnes of coal and eight million tonnes of ore, and moves about 445 million cubic metres of overburden per annum. Infrastructor operates a variety of coal and metalliferous mine sites across Australia and Indonesia, and is developing a large greenfield coal project in India through a subsidiary. Infrastructor moves more than three million tonnes of material per day.

Infrastructor projects have encompassed a broad range of minerals including coal, copper, uranium, nickel, gold, iron ore, silver, lead, zinc and magnesite. Infrastructor has extensive experience in all forms of open cut mining and dragline operations as well as dozer push mining. Infrastructor also owns, operates and maintains one of the largest, most diversified fleets of mining and construction plant in Australasia.

Regulatory environment of Infrastructor

Infrastructor is a wholly owned subsidiary of an ASX 100 public company which is subject to the requirements of the Corporations Act and ASX Listing Rules. Subsidiaries are distinct legal entities also subject to specific provisions of the *Corporations Act*.

Why Infrastructor was selected for a case study

While Infrastructor is a wholly owned subsidiary of an ASX 100 company, the company maintains an independent identity and culture from its parent company. It possesses a high level of autonomy in developing its own markets and client relationships. The company sees its core strength in its diversity and the ability to offer a whole-of-business approach to project management. This sense of autonomy and responsibility is partly evidenced by the fact that Infrastructor prepares its own detailed sustainability report, whereas its parent entity does not.

Infrastructor has an established corporate reputation as a leader in the sustainability field. This seems to be driven by two key factors:

- a strong competitive desire to be a leader in its field in a variety of areas, including sustainability
- a strong focus on the client, particularly developing long-term client relationships.

For instance, the senior environmental adviser of business services noted that Infrastructor was particularly cognisant of client trends, stating:

> I know Infrastructor likes to be a leader in the industry. If this [sustainability reporting] is what their clients are doing, they will do it as well. I have heard this called – like you have probably heard a million times – a ticket to the dance. I think it started as a HSE [health, safety and environment] report ... then it has sort of grown with the badge of sustainability, it is

> changing slightly. But it is sort of taking a long evolutionary
> path to get to where we need to go. You know I think they do
> it because they like to disclose this type of information.

Infrastructor is unique among its peers in its commitment to a wide variety of sustainability initiatives which appear to be strongly supported at all levels of management within the organisation. The manager of greenhouse and energy stated:

> I don't think there is any resistance. I think everybody's
> embracing it very much and that's the response that I get and
> I think that there is no problem, and I think there's actually
> part of the policy which we have that we are actually moving
> in that direction. That's really an important part of the
> business and a very good way forward.

The respondents indicated that there was a consistent positive message from top level management towards sustainability that has facilitated widespread buy-in across the entire organisation. The manager of greenhouse and energy stated:

> You have to demonstrate leadership in that area and in
> energy efficiency and we've never had problems with that so
> that's very, very good for us, so we have a lot of support from
> senior management. We are looking at strategies. Very early
> in the game we had a committee which looked at compliance
> and the opportunity to go in various other directions,
> which could potentially be beneficial for us in the emissions
> trading scheme. I think we have done a lot so far in preparing
> ourselves for the future.

Infrastructor was also selected for this case study on the basis of its industry background as a mining, construction and service entity. Being a mining and construction entity, Infrastructor is significantly affected by the rising challenges of a carbon-constrained economy, and is particularly sensitive to any government regulation, initiatives or proposals to limit carbon emissions (such as a carbon emission trading scheme). As stated by the manager, greenhouse and energy, 'Whatever is going to happen, one thing is always the same, we have to reduce our carbon footprint no matter what'. The mining and construction focus of the company therefore provides an interesting contrast with the four other cases examined in this book.

Respondents selected for the case study

Respondents were drawn from a wide cross-section of the organisation and involved eight interviews averaging approximately one hour each. Interviewees included respondents with the following occupations: group environmental manager, group financial accountant, senior environmental adviser, business services, manager, greenhouse and energy, group management accountant, group strategic sourcing manager, group plant manager, HR manager – corporate, executive general manager, strategic communications, and director, finance and administration.

Outline of case study

The remainder of this case analysis is organised as follows:

Section one explores some of the issues surrounding the public image of sustainability projected by Infrastructor and the perceptions of sustainability reporting by respondents working daily with the programs and initiatives within the organisation.

Section two explores Infrastructor's processes, systems and methodologies for the collection, integration and reporting of sustainability information.

Section three explores the extent to which stakeholder engagement influences or impacts on sustainability reporting practices within the organisation.

Section four discusses potential hurdles confronting the collection, integration and reporting of sustainability information within the organisation.

Finally, some conclusions and policy implications are considered.

Infrastructor management structure

Board of directors

The Infrastructor board of directors meets quarterly to review the company's financial, human resources, health and safety, environmental and community performance. Its primary objectives are to ensure Infrastructor complies with statutory obligations, oversee policy, procedures and governance and provide strategic council advice to the managing director.

Management team

The executive management team (EMT) sets out the company's overall strategic direction, and develops accountability for its regional and discipline-specific business units and functional areas. The EMT works closely with senior managers to implement business objectives and review operational performance. Executive meetings are held monthly and a broader management meeting is held quarterly. Throughout the year, the EMT assesses performance against the company business plan. This plan is updated annually, and outlines strategies and business objectives for each business unit and corporate functional support area over a three-year period. The EMT recognises the need to continue upgrading skills provides improved business support to meet the needs of the business units and expands the business capability of the company, particularly for large privatised, high-risk projects and strategic investment opportunities.

SECTION ONE

Public image versus internal perceptions

The main sustainability initiatives of Infrastructor are deeply ingrained in the organisation. The interviews with respondents suggested that Infrastructor is driven by a competitive spirit to be leaders in the field and a desire to be client focused. The commitment of Infrastructor to sustainability is supported by a number of internal initiatives within the organisation, including the preparation of a detailed sustainability report, which its parent company does not prepare. Infrastructor's 2009–10 sustainability report states its overarching philosophy to sustainability as follows:

> We aim to minimise the impact of our operations on all aspects of the environment, including air and water quality, noise levels, native flora and fauna, soil conditions, and areas of historic and cultural interest. No matter what the project, the goal is to complete it with as little impact on the environment as possible. Rehabilitation is an essential component when impact on the environment is unavoidable as part of day-to-day operations. The future of the construction, mining and services industries is inseparable from the global pursuit of sustainable development.
>
> We are working towards an environmentally sustainable future. To achieve this goal, we are actively integrating environmental management into our core business activities and environmental sustainability into our designs. To support our objectives, we are creating a renewed environmental vision – a commitment that restates our move beyond compliance towards sustainable innovation and minimising our footprint. At Infrastructor, everyone has a responsibility

not only to our projects and our company but to present and future generations to lead the way.

The philosophy of sustainability projected in the sustainability reports appears to be well supported by a variety of sustainability initiatives, which also surfaced in several of the respondent interviews. Key sustainability initiatives include: actively reducing carbon footprint, energy efficiency initiatives, and project-wide environmental innovations or 'being carbon-conscious'.

Actively reducing carbon footprint

As an integrated construction, mining and services contractor, Infrastructor openly concedes it is a major carbon polluter. However, the company claims to be committed to maximising energy efficiency and reducing greenhouse gas emissions. The 2009–10 sustainability report states:

> [We] use a greenhouse emissions and energy management information system based around our enterprise resource planning system to better measure energy use and energy production, and estimate greenhouse gas emissions. Together with rigorous data collection systems and in-depth training programs, this system enables us to collect quality data for our own analysis, our clients and the Australian Government.[3]

---

3 In its 2010 sustainability report, it is stated that Infrastructor's associated Australian and international facilities consumed 27.1 TJ of energy and emitted an estimated 1.97 MtCO2-e of greenhouse gas (GHG) in 2009–10. For the Australian facilities, there was a less than 1.5 per cent increase in 2009–10 compared to the previous period, with the increased use on large civil Infrastructor projects offset by the cessation of one mining contract. Mining activities continued to contribute about 80 per cent of the total energy use and emissions. Civil Infrastructor contributed 10.5 per cent and waste treatment facilities five per cent. Diesel

Infrastructor has also triggered the reporting thresholds for the *National Greenhouse and Energy Reporting Act* 2007 (NGER) and have reported GHG emissions and energy use for the facilities under its control since 2008–09. As a wholly owned subsidiary, reporting is conducted through the controlling corporation. In 2009–10 there were 98 facilities under its operational control and 75 under the operational control of another party.

Energy efficiency initiatives

The Australian Government's *Energy Efficiency Opportunities Act* 2006 requires large energy users to identify, evaluate and publicly report on energy saving opportunities. Although a subsidiary, Infrastructor directly manages its own participation in the program and has carried out a representative assessment of its Australian mining business in accordance with the government-approved assessment schedule. Infrastructor also participated in a voluntary assessment verification audit with the Department of Resources, Energy and Tourism with no non-compliances against the assessment principles identified.

Infrastructor appears to carry out several energy-efficiency initiatives, including:

- Reduction in mining equipment idling time
- Turbo idle downtime reduced from five to three minutes on most large equipment
- Daylight controls on mobile lighting plants
- Replacement of mobile lighting plants with equipment mounted LED lights.

---

combustion represents 95 per cent of the energy used and 75 per cent of the GHG emissions.

Project-wide environmental innovations or 'being carbon-conscious'

Infrastructor has a carbon-conscious culture, with the following specific initiatives:

- Recycling all steel waste
- Using recycled crushed concrete from demolition activities and off-site sources for use on haul roads where possible
- Using recycled concrete within the cement treated crushed concrete pavement layer on permanent roads
- Using recycled crushed bricks as aggregate for backfilling around 'green pipe'
- Mixing asphalt with 50 per cent recycled asphalt pavement (RAP) for resurfacing of car parks
- Using asphalt profilings with high RAP content on temporary construction roads
- Using 'green pipe', made from recycled materials, for selected drainage.

One initiative that came out in the interviews was policy on tyres. Infrastructor is the third largest consumer of tyres in Australia, after BHP and Rio. Tyres present unique environmental issues as they are not biodegradable and have very limited alternative uses.

The group strategic sourcing manager reiterated the company's keen interest in the environmental implications of tyre recycling, and has devoted considerable resources to addressing the issue:

> [The] focus has been put on tyres. We put a tyre manager on to allocate tyres to sites, instead of sites just interfacing with suppliers on their own. We moved from, in particular with Michelin our biggest supplier, we moved from a distributor interface right through to Michelin direct. So we're dealing

with the manufacturer. So we have relationships with those. We put our forecasts in. They know we are going to give them that information, so that they can put that in to expand their tyre production.

With respect to tyre initiatives, the manager, greenhouse and energy said, 'We were able to expand tyre life enormously which saved us a lot of money and a lot of greenhouse gases'.

The positive public image projected in the sustainability reports of Infrastructor appeared to be shared by many respondents. The manager of greenhouse and energy suggested that reducing carbon emissions was embedded in the organisational culture of Infrastructor. However, the company was facing significant challenges in achieving this goal:

Whatever is going to happen, one thing is always the same, we have to reduce our carbon footprint no matter what. We have to save energy and we have to look at all the various parts of our business whether we do this here within Australia, or whether we go abroad and have it up there, what we could do there ... I think the message which you get within Infrastructor is really look at how you can save energy, be very mindful with the resources you have available, you purchase them or whether you get them for free or whatever. Use them very carefully and reduce your carbon footprint.

We have started to have this Greenhouse Challenge Plus Champions Network and they had to come up with action plans from each and every business unit in order to show and update and quantify the emissions rate reductions. The emission rate reduction means that you use less energy ... I mean, in the long term we definitely have to have a look at what we're going to do in the future. That's definitely a challenge. We are operating in a very emissions-intensive industry and we have to closely look at whether this is sustainable in the future, whether we still can do this or maybe we have to be prepared to pay a very high price for that. Even if you pay a penalty you still have to make good, you still have to get the permits and I'm not sure whether these permits are going to be available in the future.

Other respondents were more sceptical about the realism of these initiatives. The chief financial officer expressed major doubts about the capacity of Infrastructor to influence the carbon emission policies of its clients:

We've got to look at it realistically enough though. If it's mining business, it's going to be a mining business and if the resource owner is the reporting entity and we are a mere contractor and the cost is passed through and they determine that they still want to produce so many tonnes of coal. I mean, we're not going to stand there and say we're going to drive a 20 per cent reduction elsewhere and go out of business or something. It's got to be the linkage between who the resource owner is, what they're producing – coal mainly – and the impact on us whether we are the only contractor or, you know, the owner might be doing some operations on site as well.

Furthermore, some respondents appeared to equate the concept of sustainability with efficiency concepts and measures. For instance, the group plant manager's priority in sustainability was efficiency savings and the bottom line:

It's an interesting topic because most of sustainability ... I suppose, to me, a lot of it runs back to what you say; the efficient operation of the equipment. Generally, whether it is in the maintenance or the application of it, what we are going to do to improve the sustainability is really, I think, to run that equipment as efficiently as we can and to drive our operations and operate our projects as efficiently as we can. It takes everything from the equipment maintenance to our control of our projects that affect things like our tyre lives, our fuel use. Our design of our projects affects the fuel use of the assets as well, so I think a lot of it is really based around driving the most efficient operation we can. A lot of it people say you should be doing that, anyway, because it's good for the bottom line. Sometimes I think we could improve in some of those areas.

Efficiency savings can be affected without a sustainability perspective per se. The group plant manager implied he was happy to be 'green' so long as this perspective did not cost money:

This issue of sustainability, what does it really mean? To me, it's really driving an efficient operation and all it does is highlight inefficiencies in our operation which we should be improving, anyway. You're right, we should be doing those. I think it's just another ... [indication for] our operations guys to highlight the inefficiencies where we need to be improving. So I'm not sure really what sustainability means. The most sustainable thing I think we can do is run an efficient operation ... I've said to our in-house green lobby that we're happy to be green as long as it doesn't cost us any more money. We're happy to be green if we can do it and it doesn't cost us any money.

However, it was clear from other respondents that the sustainability culture at Infrastructor was more deep rooted than a desire to improve efficiency and the bottom line. The executive general manager indicated that sustainability was more about a balance between efficiency and the environment:

> One of the values is that we're performance driven. We're not going to be an organisation that goes out and wastes money. We've got to perform but, on the other hand, we're not going to do that at the expense of killing people or destroying the environment or working with people on the take and so on. All of those kinds of considerations are important when we move into new markets overseas and new partners within Australia. All of those things are changing.

SECTION TWO

Sustainability: data collection, measurement and reporting

While claiming strong sustainability initiatives in the sustainability report, it was evident from the interviews that Infrastructor struggles with many aspects of data collection and measurement. Furthermore, any assurance of sustainability data has mainly been carried out through internal audits. It was also unclear from several respondents what specific environmental performance targets the company pursued. The most recent sustainability report of Infrastructor set out a limited number of environmental performance goals and achievements, including:

- environment performance[4]

- reducing adverse environmental incidences and ensure compliance with environmental laws.

Achievement: No Class 1 incidents were recorded. While there was an increase in minor incidents, this can be attributed to an increase in the scale of our projects.

Refine and refresh our environmental values, policies and key messages.

Achievement: This process has begun and is currently in review before being rolled out across the business.

Comply with national greenhouse and energy reporting legislation and evaluate and report publicly on our energy saving opportunities.

---

4 Infrastructor also reports on people performance, safety performance and community performance in similar terms.

Achievement: In 2009–10 our energy savings were calculated at 53,500 GJ.

Lack of clarity on targets and lack of specificity with the measurement of environmental data used to evaluate targets surfaced in several interviews with respondents. Several respondents raised concerns about the measurement of the underlying data, particularly non-financial performance indicators and measures.

The chief financial officer recommended caution when interpreting environmental data as the 'science' being used to form the estimates:

> Yes, I guess sort of our sustainability report goes out as a separate document at present, how that changes with new requirements I don't know. You've just got to be a little bit cautious about some of these things. While we're still learning we are endeavouring to do our best, I can't give you an example, but I recall how they've calculated the CO_2 equivalent of a new tyre and it was 14 point something. I just questioned some of the science behind these estimates that are being used to be honest. It's good if it serves a purpose and we refine it and get better each year, but I mean there are certain environmental sign-offs that go through our board with the year-end accounts already. It's just something that we have to address.

In terms of specific reporting of environmental information, the manager of greenhouse and energy indicated the reporting of sustainability was being driven by new regulatory requirements. For instance, he stated that reporting was moving from a more qualitative to quantitative basis mainly because of the new NGER requirements:

We have quarterly benchmarking reporting for mining operations and this includes diesel usage and we differentiate between mobile and stationary diesel because we have different emission factors ... and explosives, although this is going to change ... because we need to report explosives in a different way. Then we have quarterly reports to our holding. Up until now, we had like a qualitative reporting to do but as of the first quarter of this year we also need to report greenhouse emissions, energy use and energy production. Energy production for us means coal production. This is what we need to report on the NGER anyway which I find a bit funny, but anyway.

Many respondents indicated that the collection of environmental data was seriously lacking in several areas. For instance, the manager, greenhouse and energy pointed to the problems with existing data collection systems, such as JD Edwards (JDE). He stated that the JDE system was not set up to collect sustainability information, stating:

I think this is probably the biggest flaw because the system which we have in place, JDE, was only meant for accounting purposes, for financial data. I don't think it was set up in order to provide data for environment. At that stage, nobody thought about an emissions trading scheme. But times have changed and we have to adjust now so we have to make sure that the data quality is okay and this is going to be one of the major exercises which we do within the next two weeks and we started working on that.

Another concern raised by respondents was that the accounting function was not perceived to be well coordinated with the sustainability report and environmental data collection. The chief financial officer noted that the financial statements and sustainability report were not produced or disclosed at the same time, saying:

> If you're looking within Infrastructor, I, the CFO, don't own the sustainability report. If I did it would come out at exactly the same time as our financials, but we seem to muck around with it, so that tends to come up through another part of the organisation. It sits with the CEO and because some of these things are unclear, you know, one of our board members might have a look at it and that takes more time.

In terms of procurement data, the group strategic sourcing manager stated that procurement was not well understood within the organisation which was hampering data collection efforts:

> We're not that high in the evolutionary scale at the moment. That's what I'm trying to bring to the organisation. With the change in senior management, we have a guy who's heading up our Australian operations and he tells me he knows everything about procurement, yet when we sat down and talked last Thursday, he couldn't understand anything I said. Procurement is a changing animal and, as you know, centralisation versus decentralisation can be one flavour one year and a different flavour the next and on it goes as people roll along, along, along. I'm at the moment decentralisation, I'm all for adding a bit of centralisation to it and I was told, 'That's the Stone Age, you can't go back to that', but I'm not the one in the business that's losing money and has the free for all. So it's what fits the situation to me.

The group strategic resourcing manager said:

> Procurement just needs to be pushed up a notch in this business. It needs to be taken more seriously than it is ... we

don't get the profile that we should have, possibly because they just don't understand what we do really. When it comes to things such as when you start to talk about the P2P or B2B to them, it's like trying to interpret the Bible into Egyptian or something. When you talk about contract management tools, supplier relationship management tools, e-tendering, risk mitigation tools, repositories, templates, they don't get it. I don't get a hearing, so I don't get a budget. How do I know what we do? Because we manually get the data from JD Edwards and then we data cleanse, we cleanse it ourselves, which takes us weeks.

It was clear from many respondents that Infrastructor was struggling with the integration of sustainability data within conventional databases and software. The executive manager of systems expressed a lack of faith in environmental software to 'solve' basic data collection and integration issues. He referred to the software overload as follows:

I hear there are many software packages that are getting delivered this September, I'm just amazed. The whole world is going to be flooded with new software that's going to fix every problem that's out there, but nobody can demonstrate it to me. I've got a great maxim in life – if you can't see it, can't touch it, it doesn't exist. Smoke and mirrors are wonderful, live in Las Vegas with the illusionists. So Orion 10, they're going to do that and my attitude towards it is, hey, it's a dead horse. You don't kick [it] ... I mean the counsel for Microsoft got up in a court case in the US and gave the lecture on dead horses. What do you do with a dead horse, do you whip it harder? Do you couple a couple of dead horses up together? Or do you just do what the Indians do which is dismount and find a new horse?

In terms of integrating different databases and systems within the organisation, the manager of greenhouse and energy indicated that Infrastructor had made very little progress in this direction:

> We haven't been very far down the track. That tool might actually tap into those systems as well depending on what kind of information we are actually going to need in the future. It is envisaged that we can expand it. For instance, if you want to capture data about tyres, about loops, about water – because water is going to be the next thing which is really important for us – this system can actually manage everything which you want to add.

The information systems manager also stressed the lack of integration in systems used to collect environmental data, as well as HR, payroll and financials. This is partly a function of the organisational structure of the company. The information systems manager said:

> It's a bit of, I guess, a work in progress at the moment. It's through whatever sort of business structures we've had in the past and all the rest of it, and then we've had certain systems implemented under certain models and all the rest of it. It's been reasonably disjointed. Like, for quite a long time we've had HR, the HR department was run under a separate, I guess, executive line management to staff administration. And then you had staff administration for wages and payroll and then another staff administration group for salary payroll. And then you've got another staff administration group in Indonesia and it sort of gets more and more complex. So not only has there, I guess, been a level of brokenness in the systems, there's been a level of brokenness in the actual structures within the company. You've then only got to

realise that the drivers for a HR system are going to come out of HR, the drivers for a payroll system are going to come out of the two different payroll groups and, unfortunately, never the two will meet as far as getting a consistent view.

So the ownership for the HR system was in HR but the same systems are also then being used for wages payroll, but the people on the salary payroll were sort of getting entered into the HR system, but only as a thing they had to do. There wasn't a real, I guess, consistent strategy going forward as to how this all hangs together.

At the moment, Infrastructor has gone through some internal changes. I guess the role of HR has been re-evaluated as, too has everything else in the place. And I guess they've now formed a view that HR and admin systems and stuff should be one and the same and probably should be owned by one group and I guess we're at that point now where they're trying to work out what that all means and what system that means they should use. JD Edwards has a payroll and HR system in it. They're evaluating that as opposed to the system they've already got or outsourcing some components of it. They're looking at the cost effectiveness and all the rest of it. So, at this point in the game, I'd say integration between HR, payroll and our financial systems is pretty poor.

The executive manager of information communication technology stressed there was no cultural resistance to systems integration per se, but the problems were more of a technical nature. The respondent enforced the need for a technical framework and a strategy to render systems integration more feasible in the organisation, stating:

There are a couple of things with integration ... I guess the technology in my eyes has really only become, not necessarily user friendly, but more achievable in the last couple of years. Like prior to them, actually integrating systems, there was pretty much a point-to-point system, a whole lot of pain, if you want to integrate this system, you've got to start with that system and make it work. The whole concept of your integration layers and integration middle wares and so forth, have been around for probably five or six years but they were largely pretty poor and probably more cumbersome to actually implement than actual point-to-point solutions. That's changed fairly well in the last couple of years.

Products like your Oracle BPEL and your BizTalk Enterprise from Microsoft and all the rest of it, can actually allow you to do that. So there's been that restrictor within Infrastructor. We realistically had to upgrade our JD Edwards system to be able to let it talk to some of the newer middle wares and that was one of the driving reasons to upgrade JD Edwards. We've just gone through that upgrade sort of towards the end of last year. So the framework is there, we can actually now do some of this stuff.

I guess there has been a desire from certain parts of the business to push all this stuff together – like the classic one is the on-boarding of staff, they've got to go through several systems to get someone on the system. So I don't know that there's a lack of desire within the business to have it integrated. I think it's probably the other way. I think the actual guys out in the street are frustrated that they've got enter stuff in several systems. But I think what has been lacking is: one, the technology framework to make it achievable; and, two, the actual strategy and plan I guess to do it. This has probably been the downfall. I wouldn't put it as lack of interest.

However, the Information Systems Manager was ultimately pessimistic about the prospect of high level integration across databases:

> I guess it's like the age old sort of argument that it depends on who you talk to. But personally, I don't think you'll ever get to that point [of high level integration]. You'd need a lot of maturity within the business to get to that level and you'd need a lot of discipline in the business to get to that level and, when you're working in a company such as Infrastructor which is multi-discipline, multi-geographic locations and all the rest of it, it really flies in the face of doing that. And if you talk to any of the ERP sort of vendors, they say that we do everything about 80 per cent well. And the common argument is: do you have the discipline in the company to actually push processes and procedures on them that probably only 80 per cent fit? Or do you let the ERP system do what it does very well which is, in most cases, core financials? Some of those systems will then have modules, I guess, that they've tailor-made to fit your business and then go and put in your best of breed point solutions and integrate them.

> My, I guess, professional view is that the way that industry's going is that there's going to be more and more work going on the integrations base. And you only have to look at what the Microsofts and Oracles of the world are doing and the amount of money they're spending on integration layers. They've identified too that they can't go and build these big super systems where one system suits all people. It's

a fallacy and I really don't see how you could do it unless you're in a very simple business where you can say, 'This is the stuff we do, it's not going to change, we can build a system to suit it and be done'. With the type of company we are, where we're fairly aggressive in acquisitions, taking on new types of companies working in different spaces where we haven't worked before, you're not going to go and literally be hamstringing yourself. Yeah, we've got to do it all in JDE ... but I guess it's one of those things you keep an eye on it from the industry perspective, but yeah, probably five or six years ago it was – if you have an ERP and if the data is not in the ERP, it's not real data. But yeah, look at what the market's doing and Oracle, for instance, they've got Oracle financials, they've got PeopleSoft, they've got JDE and any other very sort of middle ware players or smaller end players in those bases. And the next version of JDE will be able to play in the middle ware and then be able to talk to Oracle Financials module. So they can then turn around and sell us an Oracle Financials thing for this, a JDE thing for that, a PeopleSoft thing for that and then look at it altogether. So that's, I guess, my view is where things are going. The argument might turn around in another four or five years, when they realise it is not easily achievable. But, at this point in the game, I don't see that. I guess the questions we have internally is where is the data best suited to be placed, and where is the majority of the data, what systems is the data already residing in?

SECTION THREE

Stakeholder engagement

Respondents provided some indication of who they perceived their major stakeholders to be. An intriguing question is why Infrastructor, a wholly owned subsidiary, prepares a separate sustainability report while its parent company does not? Who is the sustainability report targeted at? The senior environmental adviser, business services cast some light on this question. He stated:

> Who are our stakeholders? Well we send it to all our clients obviously, all our major clients and the project managers on those jobs. Industry partners, we send it to them as well. Interested parties, obviously parent company, sister companies will get it as well.

The executive general manager stated:

> Our key stakeholders externally are our clients. Certainly, our shareholders even though we have the one but in the context of our parent company and its reporting on to the wider community, we certainly have to form part of that process to the broader shareholders.

The company's employees also appeared to be a major reason for preparing a sustainability report. The executive general manager stated:

> What we know about attracting new staff is that people want to know what the organisation stands for. They want to know that it's corporately responsible. They want to know it's got a good reputation, at least the kind of people we want to employ are people who care about those things. Certainly,

for the younger generations of people it's very, very high on their list of things to tick off when they're considering whether to join this company.

SECTION FOUR

Hurdles facing the collection, integration and reporting of sustainability information

Notwithstanding that Infrastructor is an industry leader in sustainability and has developed a number of innovative sustainability initiatives within the organisation, a number of respondents identified several hurdles facing the effective collection, integration and reporting of sustainability information for decision-making.

One hurdle facing the organisation is that the parameters of sustainability itself are poorly defined, partly because the concept itself is still evolving. The executive general manager stated:

> In terms of sustainability reports, we're conscious that we have been leading the field and others are now taking up the challenge to report in that same way. I think there are fads in this arena and I'm sure you'd know more about that than I do. Having worked in the field of corporate affairs for a long time, even having sustainability being the word that is the catch-all now, is a relatively new thing and it's, for me who comes more from a communications, community relations background, it's a camp that has kind of taken over things like health and safety because everything is about sustainability.

It was clear from the interviews that Infrastructor uses a variety of systems and software packages that attempt to capture environmental data. For instance, the company was one of the first users of Greenhouse Emissions Energy Management Information System (GEEMIS). The company also used other software in anticipation of the NGER legislation, such as JDE. While the interviews indicated there was very strong management support for various sustainability initiatives within the organisation, the manager of greenhouse and energy said that the biggest obstacle to implementing environmental systems came from engendering commitment with the underlying users, stating:

> [Engendering commitment with users is] one of the major things because the biggest hurdle in implementing a software tool such as this is actually the obstacles which come from the users ... so we need to get everybody on board and tell everybody what it is all about – to avoid a duplication of systems. Everybody is going to benefit from the system because every manager will have a tool on hand which tells them exactly how much energy they have used and what it actually costs them and how many emissions were produced and how many carbon credits they need to have in order to abate that. So it provides them with a lot of information in order to best manage their exposure. In the future what it is all about is really how to manage our carbon risk and this is how we are going to be judged by companies, by our future or current clients. This is how we're going to be judged by investors so what we do in this area in managing carbon risk and managing communities, all this CSR, so this is part of it. We are very much aware of that and try to prepare as soon as possible.

A key issue surfacing in the interviews was the difficulty in collecting and measuring sustainability data effectively. The manager of greenhouse and energy stated:

> The accounting system actually doesn't produce emissions data. We just take out the volumes which are consumed and then we actually, in our department, do the calculation currently. Unfortunately it takes quite some time to get that information so the information is there, but to get it out,

that's a problem and it takes some time. That's the reason why last year we had a look at this other tool, in order to make the information a lot more easily available because it takes me about four or five weeks, depending on how much help I have to get that information, and that's just not feasible in the future. I said, 'Guys, we need to have a system in place which provides information ad hoc'.

The group management accountant made a similar point:

Basically the JDE system was dollar-driven and a couple of years ago when we were ... well, two or three years ago when we started putting all this information together, the guys in the environmental department found it very difficult to get the information so we went into JDE and we established a new method of putting that information through at the time of purchase. So we know how many litres of fuel a project wants – 200,000 litres this particular month.

With regards to procurement screening, the group strategic sourcing manager stated the manual nature of data collection and size and complexity of the transactions as:

a paper chase. We have 41 000 active suppliers on the system; there would be more if you looked at all suppliers. I think we have about 270 000 to 300 000 purchase orders a year, and that's not line items. So you're going to millions when you start with line items. We have a 34 per cent invoice rejection rate, which means that when they try to reconcile, either it hasn't been receipted in or there is no purchase order raised or they can't find a purchase order number or there is a variance. So that's a potted view, is that enough?

When asked at what point Infrastructor would consider extending the JDE systems to capture information such as energy data, the chief financial officer responded by saying:

> There is only a generic answer to that question, but it doesn't have to be JDE necessarily. We've got all sorts of systems with project management, but we are acutely aware of course of all of these greenhouse issues. The legislation isn't clear yet, the impact therefore on our clients, or Infrastructor as a contractor, is not clear yet. There are all sorts of different positions that could unfold between pass-through situations to where we have liability. Dollars will no doubt drive our desire to get accuracy.

The group strategic sourcing manager also alluded to the silo culture of Infrastructor, where 'the project manager is king', as a break on progress:

> Well we are a very silo business, given our nature. Given the types of industry that we are in, project is supreme and the project manager is the king. However, this system is also used for people to hide behind, so that's one of things that stop us being more successful. With mandated spend, and there are very few of those, there is travel, fuel, tyres etc., we have been very successful in that we have managed to interrelate with the owner groups and develop an approach. Say for tyres, for instance, when we first approached tyres it was: 'You're not touching my tyres. Bridgestone will look after me, I don't care what sort of contract you put in place, and I'm not going to honour it.' But we've come to a situation where everyone agrees that it's been a benefit. So as far as successes, we have tyres when other people don't. We can put tyres in warehouses when other people don't. Focus has

been put on tyres. We put a tyre manager on to allocate tyres to sites, instead of sites just all interfacing with suppliers on their own. We moved from, in particular with Michelin our biggest supplier, we moved from a distributor interface right through to Michelin direct. So we're dealing with the manufacturer. So we have relationships with those. We put our forecasts in. They know we are going to give them that information, so that they can put that in to expand their tyre production.

Another significant obstacle that surfaced in the interviews was lack of commitment at the board level, in terms of being active advocates for sustainability rather than being mere repositories for information. The chief financial officer stated:

We have people who are quite strong on environment and will make certain representations in public, just as part of general education awareness, whatever ... we had an outside organisation in the west come and address the board. But there really aren't initiatives being driven by particular board members. I mean we are all probably as naïve as what I'm coming across here and now. Really sitting and waiting and observing and trying to understand what we've got to do.

An issue that surfaced with many respondents was the lack of certainty over proposed or pending government regulation to limit carbon emissions, such as a carbon trading scheme. When asked, 'What do you think are the largest challenges both internally and externally to sustainability?' the manager, greenhouse and energy stated:

Externally, I really think that's the emissions trading scheme, because it's such a big uncertainty currently. The biggest problem which I currently see is actually that we need to cut down emissions tremendously and since the scheme is covered so broadly there is not much room to move. So I really don't know what the outcome is of that.

The group management accountant emphasised that the financial implications of any new regulation to limit carbon emissions were not clear:

The dollars will probably fall but the quantities, I personally probably wouldn't be interested in the quantities. I mean, it's the dollars. I know we've got these carbon credits and all that, people looking at that. As we said, we're still not too sure how that's going to happen, whether they're going to go out based on a permit-based thing where you pay for it up front in cash or whether it's going to be exchanged on the market.

Lack of awareness and initiative among mining companies also surfaced as a key obstacle to progress at the industry level. The manager of greenhouse and energy stated:

I found this actually really shocking. I'm sitting in the greenhouse group of the minerals council and just recently had a discussion with ... he's shocked about the industry, how little they actually know about what's coming up. They are not involved in discussions with the government and I honestly can't understand it because government goes out, they seek information from industry. They really want to know what's going on in industry.

The manager, greenhouse and energy also stated:

If you talk to the Department of Climate Change, sometimes I have a feeling they have no idea. They are really waiting

A case study analysis of Infrastructor

for us to provide information. Because it's the first time that they are actually involved in the process, because up until now it was mainly the US who were involved in that but now it's the Australian Government so they need to capture all the information and they need to provide us with something which works. So they go out and they liaise with industry and they want to have the information and try to get the best outcome of it.

Another potential obstacle for sustainability reporting identified by respondents was the GRI reporting requirements. Some respondents believed the GRI was not overly useful for reporting purposes. The executive general manager stated:

My background, I'm a psychologist, but I've been working in public affairs for a long time and the issue of reputation is something that I've looked at in not just a practical way but in an academic way as well. There's a sense that, if you're completely transparent on everything, you will enhance your reputation and it's not entirely true. Again, I think there's a bit of kind of factionalism around that sort of stuff. It may or may not be in the best interests of the businesses' long-term survival and when we talk about sustainability the first thing you want to have is a business that keeps going because otherwise a lot of this doesn't make a lot of sense. There are some questions that I've seen on that GRI that my initial reaction to is, I'm not sure, we'll have to think about that, if that's what it is.

Summary and conclusions

The objective of this research is to identify and evaluate the state of practice relating to the collection, integration and use of sustainability information within various public and private organisations in Australia. An extensive theoretical and empirical literature has examined disclosure demographics and potential motivations for voluntary sustainability disclosure by public companies. However, very few studies have explored the measurement and reporting of sustainability information in an internal context. The focus of the case analysis was on existing accounting systems and procedures used by organisations to generate data on non-financial performance – including physical/environmental, socio-economic and governance concepts – as well as understanding the unique hurdles each organisation faces with respect to more efficient collection and integration of sustainability reporting for decision-making and strategic planning.

The study also explored a number of ways in which sustainability data can potentially be collected more efficiently and be better integrated through the accounting system, how accounting systems could be extended to incorporate such information, and the tools required to complete these specifications. This research has also considered how internal management and decision-makers in organisations make use of sustainability information and how the data might be enhanced by expanded accounting systems.

Five major organisations were used as the basis for this study. Green Insurer is a multinational corporation listed top 40 company on the Australian stock exchange. The company is renowned as a leader in sustainability reporting, being one of the more prominent Australian public companies to support the use of the GRI. The company's sustainability report includes considerable performance data. Under the direction of an executive with a high profile in the sustainability community, the company has been developing internal systems with the ultimate aim of embedding sustainability key performance indicators (KPIs) in individual performances.

Herbal Life is a medium-sized manufacturing/pharmaceutical Australian listed company. Despite the limited availability of sustainability information provided by the company, and the relatively primitive sustainability information systems used for this purpose, the company nevertheless has an outstanding reputation in the industry as a socially responsible organisation.

Local Leader (a large local government authority) is widely perceived as a leader in sustainability management and reporting. It is actively involved in a number of initiatives on sustainability reporting.

Clear Water is a state-owned authority with the responsibility to maintain water supply for four million people. The organisation has produced a sustainability report for a number of years for which it has won reporting awards. This organisation is also noted for its innovative sustainability reporting.

Infrastructor is a construction/mining entity and an unlisted subsidiary of a multinational corporation, ultimately based in Europe. The organisation prides itself on being a leader in sustainability, which is used to differentiate it from other subsidiaries including its own parent entity. In construction it is active in pursuing green standards for Infrastructor projects as well developing a knowledge database for best practice management which includes sustainability issues.

Each organisation was selected based on their public recognition in sustainability reporting and practice, and to identify any systematic differences in measurement and reporting practices across industry groups, regulatory backgrounds and size. With respect to industry, underlying operations and activities covered finance sector, construction, water, local government and manufacturing/pharmaceutical. They range from a multinational to a local government (10 000+ employees to a couple of hundred).

Notwithstanding different industry, market and regulatory backgrounds, there were a number of similarities observable across all organisations with respect to sustainability reporting practices. There was no doubt that all organisations interviewed were strongly committed to sustainability at various levels and all had adopted a variety of significant sustainability innovations, practices and strategies. For instance, many of the respondent organisations had adopted extensive programs of recycling, had constructed or were planning to construct and lease new energy efficient 'green' buildings, were using an energy efficient fleet vehicles, had made significant progress with water consumption savings and energy monitoring, had incorporated sustainability requirements into their purchasing and supplier contracts and had clearly stated CO_2 emission targets. Many respondent organisations were using, or had at their disposal, a number of sophisticated information systems that were used to collect, store and analyse some types of sustainability information at a reasonably sophisticated level. There was also noticeable strong commitment to the underlying philosophy or ethos of sustainability across all respondent organisations which manifested in various sustainability initiatives, policies and strategies. While the viewpoints of respondents differed, sometimes quite significantly on certain issues, the interviewees shared a strong underlying belief in the 'business case' for sustainability, particularly around cost savings and attracting 'green investors'. Furthermore, many respondents believed that an emphasis on sustainability, no matter how difficult the concept is to articulate, measure and report on, was generally good for the organisation because it sent the 'right' signals to stakeholders. However, beyond the general perceptions of a commitment to sustainability, there was divergence on underlying themes with respect to the development of information collection, integration and usage necessary to support a 'sustainable organisation'. Themes that emerged include: the gap between external rhetoric and internal processes; the reliance upon formalised processes; and development of data collection systems and subsequent integration; and, the extent of external engagement.

External rhetoric: a window to internal processes?

A start point for the research, the selection of potential participants, was informed by public recognition of an organisations excellence in sustainability performance (the winning of awards for performance, reporting, etc). As a starting point it could be argued that such organisations are progressing on understanding sustainable performance, and supporting performance collection and collation of performance information.

While the initiatives were many and varied across organisations, it was clear from the interview evidence that there were instances of significant mismatch between the public rhetoric of sustainability and internal perceptions of how sustainability information was collected, integrated and reported for decision-making.

The perceived gap between external rhetoric and internal process, while at times the subject of cynicism, was also a catalyst to drive change of internal processes. Within Green Insurer a number of respondents were positioning to link the value of sustainability initiatives closely with the concept of efficiency and cost savings. However, in terms of impacts, some respondents believed Green Insurer's sustainability drive would not have substantive societal impacts until they started developing more innovative 'green' insurance products and services (rather than just 'glossy' reports).

The necessity to match rhetoric and performance was clearly an issue of concern with the organisations. At issue was the possiblity of public exposure, but equally important was that the internal response to any perceived gaps. Across the organisations many respondents clearly expressed cynicism where matching internal processes were lacking, further undermining improved sustainable performance. However, senior management in responding by seeking change the internal processes and organisation's culture to align with the external rhetoric.

Formalised processes to cultural change

The advancement of internal practices to match the external rhetoric can take a number of pathways. For organisations, such as Local Leader and Clear Water, sustainability measurement and disclosure was evolving through a formal process to regulate standard information to be inculcated into the organisation's reporting and performance culture. This should not be unexpected in large organisations seeking to embed processes to improve sustainability performance as it provides consistency and certainty in the interpretation and understanding of sustainability performance.

A key central theme for successful embedding of sustainability performance measures and reporting was the organisation's culture. However it was clear that the process of culture change varied significantly between organisations, from the formal development of data protocols and supporting technology, to extending the existing informal culture to be inclusive of sustainability performance. Clearly successful integration relies heavily upon management supporting sustainability, and sustainability being part of the 'normal' processes by which the organisation judges success.

Data collection and integration

Acceptance of cultural change to embrace sustainability for organisations is a substantial step. However, such a step is hollow without parallel change in the way the organisation measures and reports performance, and how decisions are informed. A consistent theme to emerge from the case study analysis is that all organisations were facing major issues with the collection and measurement of sustainability data, as well as integration of this data into systems and formats useful for decision-making and strategic planning. A large number of implementation hurdles were identified in this area. For instance, respondents from Green Insurer stated that the most significant obstacle to this issue was a corporate culture of resistance to change and education, particularly achieving senior executive buy in. The concept of sustainability did not seem to be well understood by the organisation in a practical sense.

Once the organisation accepts the importance of sustainability, a secondary but equally important issue of integration arises. Sustainable performance data must compete with other existing data sets for the attention of management, it must be considered to add value in the decision-making of management, and must result in outcomes that are clearly superior to the organisation. Integration faces hurdles with respect to the reliability of sustainability data, the lack of familiarity of data to potential users and the perception that it is not 'hard data' or representative of tangible improved performance. On a more practical note, existing systems that disseminate performance data supporting management systems may not in the first instance be able to capture and disseminate sustainability information. Questions over reliability and relevance therefore undermine the use of sustainability information.

External engagement

Considerable sustainability performance activities and reporting fall outside the regulated activities of the organisation. Voluntary guidelines, or stakeholder engagement may therefore be substitutes in the development of external reporting. It is noteworthy that few organisations interviewed engaged extensively with their stakeholders, or could even clearly identify stakeholders interested in sustainability disclosures.

It was somewhat unexpected to observe the limited impact of external stakeholders in driving the reporting process. With the limited insight into specific external targets and a general belief in the need to report on performance, it was surprising to find respondents within organisations identifying a gap between the external rhetoric and the actual underlying performance. But perhaps the development of such a gap plays a role as a catalyst for organisations to focus on improved processes to support sustainable performance, and thereby bridge the gap between rhetoric and reality.

Key findings

In order for sustainability to be successfully incorporated and integrated within organisations, cultural acceptance of the concept is critical. Development of a sustainability culture is best achieved through leadership or through embedding sustainability metrics in formal performance management practices.

Excellence in reporting and external engagement does not necessarily correlate with internal commitment and action toward sustainability. Hence, a 'gap' may exist between external perceptions and internal action. The recognition of such a 'gap', and anxiety over exposure, however, may act as a significant incentive to improve sustainability performance.

Beyond core regulated activities there are significant barriers facing the development of formal management systems to support sustainability initiatives within the organisation. This can be particularly acute where a strong business case for sustainability actions cannot be articulated within the organisation. Accountants and accounting conventions can potentially pose a significant barrier for sustainability initiatives because of an inherent inability to capture and analyse sustainability performance using traditional financial metrics. This may then lead to organisations extending their use and acceptance of data sources and analytical techniques as a mechanism to justify sustainability-based decisions, or simply ignore the traditional financial techniques and take a more strategic approach to sustainability.

Accountants can play a significant role in facilitating sustainability initiatives by articulating the business case for sustainability and by extending accounting technology and expertise in the measurement, collection and reporting of sustainability performance. This role is clearer within organisations that are strategically positioned to be accepted as sustainability oriented.

APPENDIX 1

OVERVIEW OF CURRENT EMS

Development

Accreditation of EMS (ISO 14000)

- Extent of accreditation
- Procedures for sites without accreditation
- Stakeholder engagement in development of EMS – corporate/site.

Data collection

Corporate level – external (need to be aware of overlap with site based reporting)

- Processes for reporting (TBL report etc)
- Targeted stakeholders – changes in importance of targeted stakeholders
- Data requirements (mandatory/voluntary) of stakeholders
- Stakeholder engagement on data needs.

Corporate level – internal

- Reports to board
- KPIs for corporate performance – format of data presented
- Changes in KPIs used over extended period – future directions of KPIs?
- Reports to EGMs/CFO/CEO
- Processes for incorporating into decision-making
- Timeliness of data collection/reporting.

Site Level

- Mechanisms for data collection
- Extent of data collection
- Timeliness of data collection
- Format of data collection
- Resourcing of data collection
- KPIs used – setting of KPIs/stakeholder engagement
- Incentives attached to performance/KPIs
- Data feedback – site level decisions versus corporate reporting.

Verification/auditing

- Undertaken – when/how often
- Internal/external verification team (accounting firm?)
- Purpose/outline
- Follow-up from the review.

Accounting systems

Index

A

B

C

Good Manufacturing Practice,
PIC/S standards of 54
government regulation 185
green buildings 10, 18, 79, 84–85,
191. *See also* green ratings
Greenhouse Challenge Plus Champions Network 123, 165
Greenhouse Emissions Energy
Management Information
System (GEEMIS) 181
greenhouse gas emissions 78–80,
94–95, 97, 118, 136,
148–149, 162, 182. *See
also* carbon: emissions
Green Insurer 9, 13–52, 189, 194
green products and services 17,
22. *See also* fuel-efficient
cars; green buildings
green ratings 10–11, 18

H

health, safety and environment
(HSE) reporting 157
Heart Research Institute 61
heating 58
Herbal Life 8, 10, 54–76, 190–191
Herbalife Eye Unit Myanmar 62
hybrid vehicles 14, 79, 85, 191. *See
also* fuel-efficient cars

I

incentives 40, 151. *See also* bonuses; remuneration
indicator owners 24, 49, 51
indicators 81, 95, 141
performance 60

Infrastructor 8, 11, 156–186,
190–191
integration 115
between systems 137, 194
high level 177
layers 176–177
middle wares 176
of information sources 139
of information systems 174–175
International Council for Local
Environmental Initiatives
(ICLEI) 88
investors 17, 73, 107, 182. *See
also* shareholders
green investors 191

K

key performance indicators (KPIs)
9–10, 24, 119, 130–131,
136, 150, 154, 190

L

legislation 120. *See also Corporations Act 2001; Energy
Efficiency Opportunities Act
2006; Local Government
Act 1993; National Greenhouse and Energy Reporting
Act 2007* (NGER); *Sarbanes-Oxley Act 2002*
legislation compliance 169
Living Smart Program 128
Local Government Act 1993 77.
See also legislation
local government council 77
Local Leader 8, 10, 77–116,
190–191

Y

www.ingramcontent.com/pod-product-compliance
Lightning Source LLC
Chambersburg PA
CBHW071547200326
41519CB00021BB/6640